Wealth Consciousness

Wealth Consciousness

A Guide from Babaji for Prosperity

Roger G. Lanphear

Authors Choice Press

San Jose New York Lincoln Shanghai

Wealth Consciousness
A Guide from Babaji for Prosperity
All Rights Reserved © 2000 by Roger G. Lanphear

Authors Choice Press
an imprint of iUniverse.com, Inc.

For information address:
iUniverse.com, Inc.
620 North 48th Street, Suite 201
Lincoln, NE 68504-3467
www.iuniverse.com

ISBN: 0-595-14068-8

Printed in the United States of America

Epigraph

"Anything I can do, you can do also, and even greater things thereof."

Jesus

Contents

List of Techniques

Preface

There is no doubt in my mind that this is knowledge of the highest order. Over the course of twenty years, these techniques to access the infinite energies of creation were revealed to me. I had no idea I was weaving together such complete and simple systems.

I know by my own life that these pages expose profound Truth. They work for me and for the people I've shared them with. This is knowledge, the likes of which can shatter archaic notions about what is human.

I wrote this book the same way I wrote three others. Without an outline, chapter headings, or even a list of topics, I sat in a quiet spot in a park, accessed wisdom using these techniques, and wrote down the words that came. The book unfolded for me logically, completely, and easily.

In fact, you can write a book the same way. These techniques cultivate prosperity while unlocking All-Knowing Intelligence. It only takes time and perseverance.

That is the key—time and perseverance. Then all that you are is yours to experience. And isn't that what prosperity really is?

The Master that gave me this book is Babaji. He is one of countless Souls who live their full human potential. He is neither better, nor more evolved. Yet he would appear to be both because he exemplifies the best that we all are.

Being fully aware of his Self, Babaji can do what seems supernatural—though in fact he exemplifies all that is natural. Having complete command over his physical body, he can change it to light and go anywhere in creation at the speed of thought. (But so can we all!!) He can appear older or younger at will. (But so can we all!!) As such, Babaji has been seen in physical bodies for eons.

Most people never experience Babaji in the flesh, but rather in their thoughts, heart, feelings, and visions. For them it is meaningless to speak of an address, or birthday, or age, or a physical description. We know little about such trivia. Instead we know about what he teaches. His only desire is to give everyone the tools to awaken full human potential.

As you get to know your Self through these lessons, you will know Babaji.

Roger Lanphear

Introduction

Even though we sometimes deny it, money is extremely powerful. Years of practicing law in Orange County taught me that, if nothing else.

Money's power became quite clear to me when I naively ran for Congress from President Nixon's home district while he was still in office. I say "naive" because I believed my ideas and solutions would capture the imagination of voters. What a rude awakening it was to discover that money, not a platform, is the true king-maker.

I remember how excited I was when a reporter from the Santa Ana Registered finally called for an interview. "How much money do you have?" That was his only question. He weighed my virtues solely by my campaign war chest. When I tried to interject my concern for the environment, the economy, or Watergate, he simply asked again, "Fine, but how much money do you have to spend?"

Needless to say, I had little money. Fund-raisers were hard to organize, and big donors only wanted to give to someone who had already attracted big bucks. It was a "catch-22": no money until you have lots of money.

I went to a few inner-circle political gatherings. That was where the elections seemed to be won or lost. That's where the kingpins of power resided. They had power because they had money.

It seemed to me that money from a select group of sugar-daddies had a strange mystique about it. It carried a punch and a power. On whichever candidate these men and women focused their money automatically fell the magical power their money bestowed.

This seemed unfair. It was baffling for the idealist I was. Above all it was demoralizing. I could see clearly that without the magic and power of money I couldn't make much of an impression with my campaign.

The lesson was far-reaching. From that moment on, I knew if I were going to make a significant mark in this world, I had to do it with the embrace of money.

But how? I had no idea how. I would like to tell you that I formulated a plan, executed it, and Lo!—there was unlimited wealth. It didn't work that way.

I knew only that I wanted to learn how to capture the power and dynamics of money. That simple desire alone seems to have been the key. Gradually, over years, the mystery unfolded. I didn't read books or take how-to courses on getting rich, manipulating markets, or leveraging. I didn't even set out with specific career goals.

Quite frankly, I didn't even know I was unraveling the mystery of money, one step at a time. Only in retrospect do I see the process I set in motion with my initial desire to learn. Nor has it ended. However, the picture is clear enough to share. Then you can join me to continue discovering the great and simple Truth about money.

I learned that each of us has the ability to attract prosperity easily and to reap the rewards only its power can deliver. Everyone has that power. I am not just speaking to the Harvard Business School graduate, but I am telling this to every human being regardless of life-style or station.

Yes, I know there are ghettos and terrible social situations that appear to breed poverty. It looks like a person's birthright often guarantees a lack of wealth.

That, my friends, is a grand illusion. It is an illusion that will tumble in this time of change. The flow of prosperity through a person's life is easy and possible for every person by virtue of being human. We each have whatever it takes to attract a flow of money. We simply need to know how. Then it will flow like water through the rapids.

Of course I am not asking you to accept this conclusion blindly. But I am asking you to keep an open mind. Read these pages carefully. Study and perfect each of the techniques. They do work. Time and practice is all that is required.

I can't over-emphasize this point: you must learn each of the exercises to get anything out of this book. If you just read these pages, you will end up with nothing. The concepts won't even make sense. You can only grasp the knowledge by direct experience. After all, what would you know about the taste of fine cuisine by only reading a cook book? The proof of the pudding is in the eating. If you are the lazy type with no intention to follow through with perseverance, give this book to someone who will.

Your resolution to learn these techniques will expose money as a form of natural energy and abundance as a natural condition. Think of several people you know who attract a steady flow of money. Don't they have something in common?

Prosperity seems to be a natural condition in wealthy people's lives. If they lost everything, in a year or so they'd be basking in money again. They have a continuous flow of wealth. It is as natural for them as water is for a river.

Money is a vital energy the well-to-do tap to manifest the great material world around them. It is just a matter of flowing with the energy, and we can all do it. To be wealthy is our natural state. If you're not experiencing abundance, you are not living naturally by flowing with the energy.

In this time of great global transformation, that concept is extremely important. To grasp it is essential before we human beings on planet earth can come to grips with poverty, imbalance of wealth, and all the ills associated with lack of abundance.

Look at nature. She is abundant—nay, extravagant. Look around. How many blades of grass do you see? How many wild flowers? How many clouds? How many snowflakes? We live in the midst of extravagance. Nature is unashamedly extravagant.

We also know that every aspect of nature is a form of energy. It is a dynamic flow of power. If you observe any small plot of nature, this flow is obvious. Seeds sprout, plants grow, flowers bloom, seeds form and fall, and the flow continues.

Money is no more, no less than an aspect of the same flow of nature's energy. This is the basic principle of this Course of Study. Money is energy. Good energy. Powerful energy. Creative energy.

By itself money has no direction. It just is. A dollar bill sitting on the table is just a dollar bill. What gives it direction is you. Your desires, attitudes, thoughts, and actions give that dollar bill a purpose. You are really the power that makes that bill something special. Lost in the forest it is nothing. In your hands it comes to life.

When I saw the power of the king-makers in California, I wasn't seeing the power of just their money. No. I was seeing the power of their focus. Their desires, their attitudes, their thoughts, and their actions put life into the dollar bills they held. Furthermore, their focus was so strong that the money they gave carried with it the gift of their power.

To be powerful requires two elements: being in the flow of the almighty energy of the cosmos and having a focus. Abundant nature is in that flow with a focus. Look at the flower—"FLOW-ER." What a perfect word! The flower symbolizes the flow of nature. It flows with all the forces around it to pollinate and create a seed. Then it returns to being a flower again. And on and on and on. It flows, and flows, and flowers. The flow is focused for its own perfect purpose to manifest another flower.

When you flow, you flower with abundance. Once this flow starts, it does not stop. It never occurs to the flower—indeed it never occurs to us either—that the flower won't go to seed to produce another flower. This is natural law: The Law of the "Flower" (pronounced flow-er).

The Law of the "Flower" is the secret for abundance. Just let go and let flow while focusing on your purpose. From this book you will learn techniques to get into the flow of the natural laws that govern money. Each of the techniques sharpens and broadens your focus. By the time you've learned them all, you will be flowing with a sharp, wide focus on a world of abundance.

In order to capture a monkey in the wild, you need only to put peanuts in a milk bottle that is anchored in place. The monkey puts her hand into the bottle, grabs a fist of peanuts, and then can't get her fist out. Of course, she could let go, but to do so would make her feel like she's lost her prize. Instead she clings and loses her freedom.

This is your choice as well. Cling to your old notions about money and remain trapped, regardless of your present wealth. Or, let go and gain freedom. Freedom with abundance is the reward for being in tune with natural forces and knowing how to focus the energy that flows through you.

Freedom with abundance is your reward for perfecting and practicing the techniques in the following pages. Learn to flow with the wealth of nature. Be a "flow-er." The flow along with a wise focus brings you lots of money for a world of plenty. Then life truly becomes fun.

We live in an infinite universe, and we have every right to experience its infinity. Prosperity is the perfect place to begin.

Part I

The Preparation

Chapter One

Rhythms of Reality

I am sitting on the grass on an island in Mission Bay at San Diego. All around there is rhythm of activity.

I can feel my heart beating and my shallow breath going in and out. I hear the whirl of helicopter blades and a distant motorcycle.

Sea gulls flap their wings to meet an offshore current, then glide down—over and over again. The tide's on its way in, only to return to the sea in a few hours. The sun is in the western sky, but tomorrow morning it will begin its cycle across the heavens again. On top of the Bajia Resort a flag flutters in a repeating pattern with the wind. The wake of a passing boat hits the shore, one wave after another.

What is all around me is constant rhythm—the easy flow of repeating actions. One sea gull now walks nearby, one foot, then the next. A sailboat silently passes, as it flows with the breeze. A bicyclist coasts by. Sea World's observation deck winds its way to the top.

Wherever we are, we experience constant rhythm of repeated actions. That is the efficient flow of energy, and we are in the midst of it. There is no way creation could exist without rhythms—from the elementary sine wave in electronics to the movements of the galaxies.

Those helicopter blades had to go around and around or the craft would fall. The pistons in the motorcycle had to keep firing again and again, or the engine would fail. The flag had to accept the wind and move with it, in and out, again and again, or it would be torn apart. The walking sea gull goes forward only by repeating the step, again and again.

Everything around us, whether from nature or man-made, uses a principle of repeating action. Without repeating action, the physical world would collapse. Rhythms are essential. Even time is a function of rhythm.

This is the most basic, the most elementary principle that brings us into the flow of wealth. All aspects of creation are involved in constant repetition. Everything is energy. The rhythm of cosmic energy is all around us as a never-ending display.

Money is an aspect of the rhythm of cosmic energy. To flow with money is to flow with nature—to flow naturally.

You begin the flow by sitting and observing like I just did. Take note of the never-ending cycles. See the repeating actions in nature, as well as in machines. Observing this lays the foundation for the flow.

This is your first instruction: *The Rhythm Response.* It is simple. Wherever you are, observe the rhythm of repeating action. See and hear the constant flow. It is always there, but you will need to look and listen. Being aware is what puts you into that flow. Quite naturally, you become a part of it.

If you're in a car, notice its wheels and moving parts repeat the same movements so it can propel you.

If you're outside, feel the breeze that is carrying the birds, or pushing a sailboat, or fluttering the flag.

If you're indoors, get immersed in the ticking of the clock, the whirl of the air conditioner, or the hum of the refrigerator.

This is such a simple procedure. It must seem totally bizarre that knowledge I dare call profound begins with such simplicity. Don't be fooled. The Law of Gravity is very simple, yet it wasn't explained until relatively recent times. That basic understanding changed the entire world. New inventions were created using Newton's discovery, and today we live a life with technology and machines that owe their existence to his explanation of gravity. It is difficult to imagine how his simple observation of falling objects could go unnoticed for so long.

The fact the earth is round and travels around the sun seems self-evident. Our modern communications with its satellites and global network would be impossible without knowing this simple truth. Yet, only a few centuries ago this fact was considered ridiculous. A powerful church actually punished people who dared suggest a round earth.

So, don't gloss over this exercise because it is so simple. The simplest are often the most hidden from view. And they are often the most useful. You'll understand this more when you experience how this body of knowledge builds on itself.

The purpose of *The Rhythm Response* is to open you to your environment. Wealth is all around you. It pulsates endlessly. Until you feel a part of it, you'll never allow it to pulsate with you and for you.

With this exercise you invite the flow of abundance. This is opening the door and hollering a welcome. It is the foundation to wallow in the vibration of money itself.

Let this exercise open your awareness to all rhythms. Wherever you go or whatever you do, be on the lookout. See the movements, actions, rhythms, and cycles all around you. Feel a part of them. Identify with them. Eventually you will look at your world with a fresh appreciation.

THE RHYTHM RESPONSE

Look around and make a mental note of all the repeating actions. It can be man-made rhythms like motors and music. It can be rhythms of your body like breath, heartbeats, or walking. It can be from nature like birds flying and leaves waving. It can even be larger cycles like seasons, days, and tides.

Do this several times before moving on to the next chapter.

Chapter Two

The Basic Practice

When you experienced *The Rhythm Response*, did you become aware of your own rhythms? If you did, I'll bet it was the first time you've zeroed in on them. Most people go a lifetime without ever noticing.

You have now experienced how creation is made up of repeating rhythms. You detected them in your home, the car, at work, in the park—wherever you were. Some were as simple as the ticking of a clock, the waving of leaves, the fluttering of a kite's tail, the thunder of a jet plane, the wail of a siren, or the cries of a baby.

Other rhythms may have been more subtle. You might have focused on the twinkling of stars, heat waves rising from a furnace, or waves of color and shadows. Perhaps you jumped to the awareness of macro-rhythms, like seasons, tides, drought and wet periods, or even ages measured in eons.

If you're scientific, your thoughts might have gone to the micro-world represented by the whirl of electrons, the pulsation of bacteria, the exactness of photosynthesis, or the constant waves of cosmic energy bombarding our atmosphere.

This is your environment, and when you respond to its rhythms, you capture its power. To become aware of that dynamic flow of cosmic energy in an infinite variety of forms is to claim your role in the scheme of nature. You are, of course, already a part of it. You don't need to do anything to enter the dynamic and constant rhythm of cosmic life. When you claim your role, you invite all that nature represents to work with and for you. When you ignore the ebb and flow of energy and activity around you, for the most part you separate yourself from it. You're opting to go alone.

Independence can be fine. Our own creativity is to be encouraged. Our own accomplishments are to be applauded. But how foolish we'd be to go into the restaurant business and ignore all the resources around us—the supply houses, the designers, the bankers, the sign makers, food wholesalers, the recipe books, the waiters, the chefs, and so on. We wouldn't shun the basic resources in putting together our restaurant. Yet when we think about bringing money into our lives we readily cut ourselves off from a basic resource for our wealth: that ever-present rhythm of everything in creation.

When we focus on those rhythms and when we respond by feeling them to be a part of us, we inherit their energy. Rhythms of the wind are never-ending. Waves of the ocean are perpetual. All activity around us constantly moves in simple, observable patterns we can respond to.

Wealth can flow naturally to you from cosmic energy. Even though they may not understand the dynamics, wealthy people are in tune with this energy that manifests abundance in countless forms for their use.

Your experience of wealth flowing from natural energy becomes clearer as you go through this book and incorporate the techniques into your life. For now, simply grasp the concept—you don't even have to believe it—just grasp the concept that making money is related to being in tune with life's constant and repeating rhythms.

Being in tune with the rhythms of reality sets you up to mold the extravagance of nature into your own wealth. Awareness of rhythms is the first step, particularly awareness of your own rhythms. In *The Rhythm Response* did you feel your own rhythms? They're there.

Body rhythms are varied and many. There's the heartbeat and the breath. Your eyes blink, and you may have a twitch someplace. Your stomach and intestines can be felt pulsating. You might even hear buzzing in your ear. The possibilities are limitless. We all have rhythms. They come and go, but at any one time several are always there. They are the hallmark of being alive.

If you haven't spent time alone just to experience the rhythms of your own self, do so now.

Continue to develop your awareness of all that is around you. Every fleeting moment notice the rhythms. Include your appreciation of the macro-rhythms, like seasons, ages, tides, and the movement of the heavens. Include the micro-rhythms in biology, physics, and chemistry. And, of course, include an awareness of your personal rhythms.

Respond to all the varied rhythms with a feeling of belonging to whatever is happening around you. This should become so natural that you won't give it a second thought.

When you have reached that point, you are ready for a technique to put you in touch with a specific rhythm that is your vehicle for wealth—your money rhythm. This is your foundation for everything else you'll learn. Without it, you can't go forward. With it, you open the floodgates for all the wealth nature bestows and you correctly invite.

Your money rhythm is unique to you. To find out what it is, follow the simple procedure I'm going to give you. Some of you might learn your rhythm the first time you try the technique. Others of you may need to try it several times. Don't fret over this. The number of times it takes does not reflect on how smart you are, or how spiritual, or how anything.

I have observed that the use of recreational drugs tends to make it more difficult to experience your money rhythm. I strongly urge you not to use drugs unless prescribed by your doctor. It is very important to keep your body and nervous system as clean and clear as possible. After all, you are going to observe a body rhythm with your body senses. It is a natural rhythm you'll be observing, and a natural nervous system will perceive it best.

Your money rhythm is your funding foundation. Your desire in life is to fund all your projects and desires. That's the purpose of money. It will naturally flow to you when you have such a foundation; conversely, money hardly flows without such a foundation. That is universal Truth.

People who experience wealth are in tune with such a funding foundation, but they may not know it for what it is. A well developed money rhythm might be so subtle that it could not be noticed without trained insight.

Discovering Your Money Rhythm is a four step technique to reveal your own money rhythm. Memorize the steps because you won't be able to look at notes.

Before beginning step One, arrange not to be disturbed for forty minutes: disconnect the phone, put the dogs out, have someone else care for the children, and lock the outside doors. Then sit comfortably in a quiet place and close your eyes. After a minute or so, connect your breathing. That is, allow no space between the in and out breaths. The breath is like a huge wheel; it just carries itself. Continue this connected breathing for about ten minutes. If thoughts are there, that's okay; just also keep an awareness of your connected breathing. If you find yourself totally absorbed in thoughts, gently return to an awareness of your connected breathing.

Step Two is also ten minutes. The connected breathing has relaxed you, and you feel settled down. Now you can breath normally. At the same time allow your attention to go to the heart region. Do you notice a pulsation in the heart region that is not from the heart beat? Feel your pulse if you aren't sure. When you do notice a pulsation that is in the heart region but not from the heart beat, allow your attention to be with it for the rest of this segment. As in the first step, don't try to push out thoughts. Just slightly favor your awareness of the pulsation.

Step Three is ten minutes, making all three of these steps the same length. Regardless of whether or not you became aware of a heart pulsation that is not a heart beat, now look for a more physical money rhythm. It can be a movement of the head around in circles, side to side, or front to back. It can be a swaying of the back, so free your back so it can move. Arms, fingers, or legs can move. Eye lids can flutter. You might see patterns of light, or your might hear a sound, or you might feel a sensation. This physical money rhythm can be anything you can notice. The only requirements are that it is pleasant and that it is something you easily sense. It might even turn out to be something you are quite familiar with. When the experience comes, focus your attention on it for the remainder of the ten minutes.

Step Four is ten minutes to lie down and rest. This is important. You get more relaxed than you realize, and you ask your nervous system to become keenly aware. If you jump back into activity without resting, you might feel irritable or even sick. So rest, stretch, and come out of the deep relaxation slowly.

That's the simple procedure for locating your money rhythm. There are four ten minute segments. The first is connected breathing. The second is to notice a money rhythm in the form of a pulsation in the heart region that is not from the heart beat. The third is to notice a physical money rhythm, and the fourth is to rest.

Your money rhythm can be the pulsation in the heart region that isn't from the heart beat, a more physical movement, or both. Most of you will eventually notice both. If you only get one and you feel quite comfortable with it, that's fine.

Invest in a journal. You will need it for nearly all the techniques you're going to learn. In the journal write a description of your money rhythms, whether a pulsation somewhere, a movement, or a sensation. Whenever you notice a change in your money rhythms, including refinements that can take place during the practice, make an entry about the change. This journal is a very important running account of your experiences and progress.

When you have a clear money rhythm down pat, incorporate it into a twice daily routine called *The Basic Practice*. Before breakfast and before dinner for ten to twenty minutes each, sit comfortably with your eyes closed and allow your awareness to be with your money rhythm; it may take a couple of minutes for the rhythm to appear. It is all right to have other thoughts and to be aware of sounds and your body. Just slightly favor the awareness of your money rhythm.

Your rhythm will change during the session. It can change tempo, get longer or shorter, or become so subtle as to almost disappear. It could even disappear while you might feel asleep. Let any changes happen; just be a silent observer. You might find yourself totally absorbed in thoughts with no rhythm. When you realize that, just return to the rhythm. These are all perfectly normal and part of the practice.

After ten to twenty minutes, take a couple of minutes to come out of the deep relaxation slowly. Not to do so may cause you to feel irritable.

The object of *The Basic Practice* is to bring wealth into your life, but this one technique opens up other incredible avenues. Some of these we'll explore in this book. Others you'll discover on your own. However, the flow of wealth that comes should be enough incentive to be regular in the twice daily practice.

Don't be in a hurry to move on to the next chapter until you feel comfortable with *The Basic Practice.* Take plenty of time to develop this technique carefully and solidly. In the following pages you'll add new layers. *The Basic Practice* is the cornerstone around which everything else is built.

DISCOVERING THE MONEY RHYTHM

STEP ONE: 10 minutes. Sit comfortably with closed eyes and let your awareness be with connected breathing—that is, allow no space between the in and out breaths.

STEP TWO: 10 minutes. With normal breathing, notice a pulsation in the heart region that is not from the heart beat. That is your money rhythm.

STEP THREE: 10 minutes. Notice a physical rhythm that is pleasant in the form of a movement, sensation, or vision. That is also your money rhythm. Allow your awareness to be with it.

STEP FOUR: 10 minutes. Lie down and rest.

THE BASIC PRACTICE

STEP ONE: Sit comfortably with closed eyes and allow the money rhythm to appear; it may take a couple of minutes.

STEP TWO: For ten to twenty minutes allow your attention to be with your money rhythm along with any other thoughts. Allow the rhythm to change tempo, get longer or shorter, become more subtle, or even disappear.

STEP THREE: Take a couple of minutes to come out of the deep relaxation slowly; not to do so may cause you to feel irritable.

Chapter Three

The Basis for Answers

Your own particular money rhythm is like a thumb print. It is unique to you. It might appear quite ordinary or exactly like someone else's, but it is one of a kind. The subtle differences between money rhythms might not even be detectable, but they are there.

Actually, *The Basic Practice* of sitting quietly and being aware of the money rhythm is one of the most valuable disciplines you can do. This puts you in direct touch with the most fundamental energy, which is your true essence.

Some of you might call that essence your soul. Others think of it as their Self. Scientists might label it a life force. Whatever you name it makes no difference. This is the energy that gives you life.

All of inanimate creation is vibration. Physics and chemistry teach that. All of life is also a vibration—a repeating action, a rhythm. You are unique in all the world. Your vibration is unique.

Everything around you is vibrating. Your vibration influences all of it, as indeed you are affected by the other vibrations. The closer you are, the more the influence.

The Basic Practice opens your conscious awareness to your own essence. You become aware that you are a vibrating being, and you feel its vibration. That conscious awareness of your basic nature is the first step in claiming all you are entitled to. And that, my friend, is all the wealth represented by all the vibrations. It is your birthright.

The Basic Practice is the key. It connects you to your essence and to all the vibrating wealth. Connected and in tune, the opportunities to make money flow to you. When you are not, you will not attract what is justly yours. It is that simple!

Some people are always in tune, and we see how easily wealth flows to them. Others struggle, work their fingers to the bone for long hours, and never get ahead. The necessity of being in tune is hardly understood, let alone believed. It appears arbitrary that some people attract wealth, while others don't.

Perhaps genetics makes it easier for some children to plop into their vibration and stay there. Perhaps family or even ethnic traditions bring this about. Maybe it's personality, or values, or determination. Whatever it is, some people are reaping the rewards. Others aren't. Indeed, so few are claiming the rewards that the spoils are going to only a few.

The principle is well known: like attracts like. Wealth gravitates to harmonious vibrations. So, the key is to get in tune with the vibration that will attract wealth. *The Basic Practice* does that.

A cursory glance around the world shows what an imbalance has come about. People are not attracting the wealth they are capable of having by their nature.

This imbalance is often thought to be a direct result of government policies, taxing regulations, social conditioning, or innate abilities. It has never been thought to be a result of how each person attracts or repels wealth with their vibration. But that is precisely what it is.

Each person on this planet has the tools to bring about a life of abundance. The only tools needed are the money rhythm and time to devote to it. With them everyone can attract a life of abundance.

"But there's not enough wealth for everyone," you might argue. Nonsense. Properly used, there is an abundance of resources here. Wisely distributed, there is enough for every man, woman, and child on planet earth to enjoy life, to contribute to society, and to experience abundance without destroying and depleting natural resources.

You have set yourself up to prove this technology. Just faithfully continue *The Basic Practice* twice daily, adding to it as these chapters unfold. You'll prove this works for you, and you will also see the solution to many social ills. The possibilities for mankind will astound your imagination.

Since your money rhythm is your own unique and basic vibration, you are actually in tune with your most inner core. That inner core isn't a place, as such. It is more a subtle and refined energy level where you are in harmony with all the resources of your environment. Then you are open for wealth to flow to you. Then you can successfully create and experience abundance.

You were made to be a creator. That's where the fun is. Nothing would be more boring than being a wealthy Rip Van Winkle. So, instead of sitting around and being bored, you're going to develop the skills of a master creator. You're going to attract the kind and amount of wealth you want and need.

In order to do this, you need a set of signals: a "Yes" signal and a "No" signal. This will give you the ability to ask any question that is relevant to your life and to get an answer.

These signals are marvelous tools to get all the answers you need to create abundance. You can guide yourself into the perfect activities to make money while contributing to a better planet.

You'll learn later how to use the signals. For now, suffice it to say that these signals are a tool. They do not rob you of decision making. You use them to identify your choices. It wouldn't be fun creating wealth if you were told everything to do. Instead you only want to learn your wisest options, and you want to avoid pitfalls. In this way you don't weaken your free will. Instead you strengthen it with sure-fire choices.

So, the next technique is to discover and feel comfortable with a "Yes" signal and a "No" signal. Each signal is a vibration similar to what you experience with the money rhythm. It can be a movement someplace, such as the head, arms, legs, or fingers. It can be a vision or a sensation. My "Yes" signal is my head nodding three times. For the "No" signal my head moves from center to left once. It can be anything that is pleasant and easily noticed.

The four step procedure for getting these two signals is simple. Step One is just *The Basic Practice* for ten minutes.

In Step Two ask for a "Yes" signal. When it comes, practice several times until you feel quite comfortable with it.

In Step Three ask for a "No" signal. When it comes, practice several times. Step Four is just practice. Randomly ask for "Yes" and "No" signals.

The total time of each session for all four steps is twenty minutes. It may take several sessions to discover and feel comfortable with both signals. Don't feel rushed.

Do not ask questions yet. You'll learn how to use your signals when you put them to use in several other techniques. For now, just be content to discover them.

This is another milestone in your gallop toward abundance. With this new technique for getting answers, you will break through barriers to create abundance for yourself and a better planet for everyone. At the same time you'll have fun making decisions and being a true creator. Isn't that the real reason for living?

DISCOVERING "YES" AND "NO" SIGNALS

STEP ONE: Begin with ten minutes of The Basic Practice: your awareness with your money rhythm.

STEP TWO: Ask for a "Yes" signal, which is a pleasant movement, vision, or sensation that you can easily notice. Practice several times until you feel comfortable with it.

STEP THREE: Ask for a "No" signal, which is also a movement, vision, or sensation. Practice several times until you feel comfortable with it.
STEP FOUR: Practice by randomly asking for "Yes" and "No" signals. The total time of each session for all four steps is twenty minutes.

Chapter Four

Correcting Subconscious Beliefs

The implications of what you've just learned are staggering. With a little more instruction and practice, you will be able to get all the answers you need to manifest great abundance. That alone is astonishing. It is incredible that each of us has access to all knowledge, but this is the simple truth.

Even with as little as we know about the brain, we marvel at its complexity. The countless miles of nerves, the infinite connections, the delicate chemistry, the role of genetics, the specialized compartments and functions are only openers. We know we have just begun to understand—if we can even use that word—how the brain fits into the whole scheme of creation.

One day biologists and psychologists will discover the brain is only one piece of a greater marvel. The brain will be considered akin to a large transformer in a power substation where energy arrives to be transformed into useful current.

In similar fashion, the brain is connected to a source of infinite intelligence, and it transforms it into useful knowledge. Intelligence is an aspect of energy. It is ordered, specific, and carries codes or information that can be read and understood by the brain.

This intelligence permeates all of creation. There is no way to escape it. Because we are part of creation, of nature, we wallow in that sea of intelligence. This is the same intelligence that comes up with the infinite variety of DNA and the life forms it produces. It is the same intelligence that keeps planets in perfect order, brings about seasons, blends earth, air, fire, and water, and struggles to preserve the balance of nature. Nothing is not touched by this intelligence because nothing is not from this intelligence.

Catch that last sentence: nothing is not touched by this intelligence because nothing is not from this intelligence. Intelligence has made everything. Everything is from intelligence. Whatever appears in creation is really just a product of intelligence. Everything came from the same intelligence.

You are that intelligence. You were created by it—whether at birth, or inception, or eons ago is immaterial. You are now created, and you have retained the intelligence that created you.

That is key. By retaining the intelligence that created you, you retain its qualities, its powers, and its properties. All the intelligence of the cosmos is retained in you. That is why you can develop techniques to learn anything you need to know. That is why your brain responds and gives you "Yes" and "No" signals to tap into that intelligence.

It is the *need to know* that governs. But what do you *need to know*? You need to know your role in preserving order, how to evolve with the natural scheme of things, how to develop your innate qualities, and how to get in touch with your nature. For these purposes you can be all-knowing.

Humankind forgot long ago these were the ultimate purposes of our precious lives. Since our link to infinite intelligence is strictly for advancing those ultimate purposes, the link was not used and withered. Instead, we embarked on power trips, on selfish hoarding, on wars, and on anger.

We lost touch with the guiding light of intelligence. Without the guide, we lost direction. Now life is a struggle. Poverty flourishes. Sickness ensues. Unfairness is everywhere.

When we lost touch with our innate intelligence, we lost our abundance, money, and the multifarious forms of wealth. That is where most of us are now. We are in a vast lake of water, yet dying from thirst. We are floating in intelligence that can guide us to our birthright of wealth. Whether or not we see that, accept it, and allow it to become part of our life is up to each of us individually. We each have free-will to accept or reject.

You may not understand fully the mechanics of how cosmic intelligence fits into our lives, how we were created by it, how it remains a part of us, or how we accept or reject its properties. It isn't important that you do. Nevertheless, you have experienced your connection to it with your "Yes" and "No" signals.

When you asked for the "Yes", then the "No" signal, you were essentially asking to be connected to that intelligence. That is the first step. The phone lines are in. Now it is time to learn how to use the line.

Incidentally, the phone is on a party line. You do not have exclusive use of the line. Everyone else has the very same right. That's important for you to keep in mind as this knowledge unfolds. Some people tend to feel better, or more developed, or special when these techniques are learned. If those thoughts start to creep in, let them go. You are indeed unique and special. However, everyone else has the same access to the same intelligence of the cosmos that you have.

In the next exercises you practice accessing this intelligence to discover knowledge you *need to know*. This book sets out a path to garner money, but by now you may suspect that your new techniques will open up far more. That be as it may, let's refocus now on money. Yeah—money!!

We all want money, Right? Well, yes and no. You may indeed think you want money, but there could be some deep-seated fear about getting it. Maybe you are afraid your friends will think you're too uppity and leave you. Maybe you're afraid to manage it—all those investment decisions. Maybe you're afraid you'll loose your ambition, or that your personality will change. Maybe you're afraid money will make it impossible to continue your career.

If you don't experience abundance, you can be certain you have some deep fear about having money. It represents pain to you. I realize that is not what you think you think. Consciously you want money and you can see all the benefits it could bring. Nevertheless, if you don't now experience abundance, you have some deep-seated fear that you need to come to grips with.

Subconscious thoughts can be a real thorn in each of our lives. They lie below the surface and scream at us. We aren't able to hear them clearly, but some part of our brain does. Whenever the brain is about to feed us a thought on what to do next, it may hear one of these subconscious thoughts.

Let us say you are approached by a friend to go into a partnership to make art posters. It sounds like minimal risk, a good return, little capital requirements, and even fun. You're about to yell "Yes" when the brain hears "I think I'd be happier without money; money is the root of all evil; it is easier for a rich man to go through the eye of a needle than enter the gates of heaven." So, you're fed a feeling of fear by your brain, and you pass up the opportunity to make the investment. You don't know why, and you may never know. You just can't.

These subconscious thoughts can torpedo each and every safe and clear chance to make money. They do, and they will. They will torpedo as long as they are there. I am not saying anything new. Psychologists have known for decades the role our subconscious plays. All kinds of therapies have been developed to get down there, see them, tear them out, relive the experience that put them there, and replace them. Each of these therapies has its place, and certainly, each has contributed to our understanding about the role of our subconscious beliefs. Now you're going to experience a very easy technique that can revolutionize all approaches for dealing with the subconscious.

You are going to ask that all-knowing intelligence within you what beliefs you have that interfere with making money. Then you're going to erase that belief and replace it with a more appropriate one. This is the first task of your "Yes" and "No" signals. It will work because this is knowledge you *need to know* to accomplish your ultimate purposes.

The six step procedure is called *The Subconscious Cleansing*. Memorize the steps before beginning.

Step One is ten minutes of *The Basic Practice* focusing on your money rhythm.

In Step Two think, "Give me a subconscious belief I have that interferes with making money." Listen for the answer. It will appear in your mind as any other thought. When you have it, ask, "Do I have a false belief that (then state it)?"

If your "Yes" and "No" signals verify the false belief, write it down in your journal, labeled *"False"*. That is Step Three.

In Step Four close your eyes again and get settled down. Then ask, "What is the correct belief?" Use the same procedure to find out and verify the correct belief. When you have it, write it in your journal next to the false belief, and label it *"Truth"*.

Step Five is repeating the process for about ten minutes. Take a couple of minutes and come out slowly to avoid roughness.

Repeat *The Subconscious Cleansing* twice a day for the next few days until you're certain you've discovered all of the false beliefs and corrected them.

This is an exercise you'll need to repeat periodically the rest of your life. New levels of beliefs surface to be cleansed, and false beliefs find their way in. Stay on top of it. Make certain you always have in your subconscious mind beliefs that support wealth.

You can correct your beliefs easily because you are in charge of your subconscious mind. It is your servant. You place beliefs into your subconscious because you think they are very important and true. You want them to override whatever else you think, without rethinking them each time. That is why you program them as automatic thinking. It is quite an efficient system as long as the beliefs are correct and serve you well.

Since you put the beliefs in the subconscious mind, you can change them. Changing the subconscious is like changing any computer: erase the old, put in the new. You do this with your *intention*. It is just a matter of intending. What you intend to believe is what will appear in the subconscious mind.

To be certain that your intention is perfectly clear, create a kind of ceremony to destroy the false belief. This is Step Six. Any ceremony that seems most fun and meaningful is fine. Keep in mind you are showing your brain what is your intention. I write the false belief on a piece of paper, then burn it. Put on your creative hat and come up with something very special just for you.

After you have destroyed the old belief, do something similar for the correct belief—the Truth—to exalt it. Some people write it down and place it on the bathroom mirror or the refrigerator. Others put it in a bible or other holy book. Writing it in your journal may be enough. Whatever you do is just to signify your intention.

There you have it. In one big swoop you can discover a false belief that limits money in your life. In another swoop you can correct the belief with Truth.

This is the first concrete step toward making money. More importantly, this is the first step in using the intelligence you are—the intelligence of the cosmos. You are created to live a life of abundance, and the intelligence behind all of creation is there to assist. Go for it.

THE SUBCONSCIOUS CLEANSING

STEP ONE: Ten minutes of The Basic Practice of focusing on the money rhythm.

STEP TWO: Think, "Give me a subconscious belief I have that interferes with making money." Listen for the answer. It will appear in your mind as any other thought. When you have it, ask, "Do I have a false belief that (then state it)?" Use your "Yes" and "No" signals to help receive the answer.

STEP THREE: Write down the false belief in your journal, labeling it "False."

STEP FOUR: Close your eyes again and get settled down. Then ask "What is the correct belief?" Use the same procedure to find out and verify the correct belief. Write it down in your journal next to the false belief, and label it "Truth."

STEP FIVE: Repeat the procedure for ten minutes. Then take another few minutes to come out slowly.

STEP SIX: Devise a ceremony to emphasize your intention to destroy the false belief and to replace it with a correct belief—the Truth.

Chapter Five

A New Belief System

You have begun to experience infinite intelligence. You asked a question, and you got an answer. In all likelihood you learned about a false belief you would not have guessed you held.

Answering questions that can help you make money is certainly worthwhile, but don't forget you are also embarking on an even more profound Course. You are strengthening your ever-present tie to the most powerful aspect of creation.

It might appear that the intelligence you tap and the answers you get come from "someplace out there." I've taught people who insisted they contacted what they call *God*. Often people think they are being guided by their *Guardian Angel* or some disembodied spirit. It won't hurt if you feel more comfortable with that explanation, but the Truth is both simpler and more profound: you are tapping your own intelligence.

There are many compartments to your intelligence. One is for what you are taught in school, such as math, biology, reading, writing, etc. Then there's what you experience: the heat of fire, the warmth of a hug, or the wetness of water. There is also a compartment for your beliefs on nearly every subject.

A fourth compartment of your intelligence knows all that the giant cosmic computer knows. No less than all the trillions of laws of nature are in that compartment.

Yes, the laws of nature are embedded into your mind as part of your intelligence because you are part of cosmic intelligence. You were created by nature and her intelligence. So were the distant galaxies as well as your pet dog created by that intelligence. Each creature, each blade of grass, and each star has all the intelligence available for all it *needs to know.*

That intelligence is like an atmosphere around you. Just as you breathe the air you need, you access whatever knowledge you need. Just as we all share the air, we all share the sea of knowledge we are all a part of.

That sea of intelligence can be polluted, just like we can pollute the air around our planet. And indeed we have done both!

Let me explain. We all bath in the same intelligence, and we all have thoughts. Knowledge comes to each of us in our thoughts from that infinite ocean of intelligence. Everyone's thoughts are connected there. What each of us believes is broadcast for everyone else to hear in this common vat. Some thoughts that are broadcast are thoughts that contradict Truth. Nevertheless, they are broadcast, and they are there for other people to hear or think.

When you think a thought, it is difficult—nay, nearly impossible—to know whether you're picking up on Truth, false thoughts floating around, or a thought all your own you just created. A thought of any kind appears only as a thought. It doesn't come color-coded.

Each of us has at one time or another picked up on someone else's thoughts. It can happen any time, but we frequently notice it when we are in love: "We just seem to know what the other is thinking." You're heard and possibly said that, I'm sure.

When large numbers of people think thoughts that are not in tune with nature, natural law, the natural scheme of things, Truth—call it what you want—then the beautiful sea of intelligence around us is polluted. It is permeated and overlaid with false beliefs.

These false beliefs do not change or distort Truth in the least. It is still there for us to access what we need. However, the Truth might get drowned out by a louder voice, like one radio signal can drown out another.

For instance, if huge numbers of people hold a particular false belief, such as "Blacks by their makeup aren't as smart and can't make as much money," then that idea gets very loud. The Truth that Blacks have the same innate potential as all humans might be drowned out.

This phenomenon explains the prejudices that permeate societies. It explains how whole races can irrationally hate another. It explains how people are pulled down or brought up by the social consciousness of their country.

When it comes to beliefs about making money or wealth, the influence of false societal beliefs is unfortunate. In many societies there is a general attitude that they'll always be poor. These are the have-not countries, and hardly anything seems to infuse energy into their economy; certainly, we've proven that loans and grants aren't enough. Other countries are wealthy, and you sense a societal belief that wealth is their condition and always will be.

The beliefs of our society definitely become our liability or our asset. Before anyone can flow with prosperity, he or she must believe and expect to be prosperous. In later chapters we'll examine in more detail how your thoughts are the beginning of your money making. As a foundation for that beginning you need to prepare your own thoughts.

In the last chapter you began that process. You discovered some of your beliefs that kept you from experiencing wealth. You didn't need to guess what they were. In fact you learned you couldn't have come up with many of your false beliefs by trying to figure them out. You have to dive into the infinite sea of intelligence for the answers. The process is simple, and it works.

Now you're going to do the same to discover the false beliefs that are held by your society and that separate you from the abundance you want and deserve. You might find that you believe "there isn't enough for everyone." Or you might uncover that "only those born into wealth are entitled to be a member of that class." A common societal belief is that "hard, hard work is the only key to success and money." If any of these beliefs are yours, reexamine it. They are not Truth.

Before you can manifest wealth, you must hold the correct beliefs. This requires that you shake away the false beliefs you hold in common with those around you.

The technique to do this is similar to the last one. It is called *Cleansing Societal Beliefs,* and it has five steps.

Step One is *The Basic Practice* for about ten minutes.

In Step Two ask, "What false belief from mass-consciousness interferes with my prosperity?" The belief will come to you as an ordinary thought. When you have it, ask, "Is the belief that (state it) a false belief in mass-consciousness?" Get the answer using your "Yes" and "No" signals. If "Yes", write the false belief in your journal labeled *"False."*

Step Three is finding out the correct belief using the same procedure. When you have it, write it in your journal labeled *"Truth."*

Step Four is repeating this procedure for about ten minutes to uncover more false beliefs in mass-consciousness and Truth to replace them.

Using the ceremony you devised in the last technique, destroy the false beliefs and incorporate the Truth into your consciousness. This is Step Five.

Continue this procedure for several days until you've uncovered all the false beliefs in mass-consciousness that inhibit your experience of wealth. From time to time check to make sure new false beliefs haven't crept in. Be vigilant the rest of your life, since we are constantly surrounded by so many false notions.

Here is an opportunity for a group experience. Any number of you that has discovered a money rhythm and the "Yes" and "No" signals can do this together. Start the same way: ten minutes of *The Basic Practice.* In the second ten minutes, share the false beliefs and Truth that come and put write them down labeled *"Truth"* or *"False."* Then devise a group ceremony to destroy the false beliefs and incorporate the Truth. You may be surprised how many of you share false beliefs.

There is far more power in even one person changing a false belief than you can imagine. When you change your thinking, you weaken the power of the false beliefs in mass-consciousness. It takes but a ray of light to dispel darkness. False beliefs do not have support from the foundations of creation. Although they are heard by everyone and affect their thinking, false beliefs do not carry much energy. Their strength comes from large numbers. Thoughts and beliefs that are in harmony with creation have much more power. One Truth can obliterate scores of false beliefs.

That is simply the way it is. Truth is far more potent than untruth. When you replace your own false beliefs with those that are supported by cosmic intelligence, the effect is felt to some degree around the globe. One person can and does make a difference.

When you reap wealth your whole society benefits. This technique *Cleansing Societal Beliefs* pulls up the whole country while it makes you wealthier.

You can't flow with wealth alone. When you flow, you're going to elevate a lot of people with you as well. You can't correct your thinking and flow with wealth without also making major changes in mass-consciousness. It naturally follows. We are all connected.

By bringing abundance into your life, you help usher in abundance for everyone.

CLEANSING SOCIETAL BELIEFS

STEP ONE: Ten minutes of The Basic Practice of focusing on the money rhythm.

STEP TWO: Think, "Give me a belief from mass-consciousness that interferes with my prosperity." Listen for the answer. It will appear as any other thought. When you think you have it, ask, "Does mass-consciousness have a false belief that (then state it)?" Use your "Yes" and "No" signals to get the answer to that question. Write down the false belief in your journal, labeled "False."

*   STEP THREE: Close your eyes again and get settled down. Then ask "What is the Truth?" When you get the answer and verify it, write it down in your journal, labeled "Truth."*

*   STEP FOUR: Repeat the procedure to get more false beliefs and Truth. The total time for steps one through four should be about twenty minutes.*

*   STEP FIVE: Devise a ceremony to destroy the false belief in mass-consciousness and replace it with Truth.*

Chapter Six

Coming to Grips With Fear

In the last two chapters you dove into your inner-most beliefs about wealth. Some were related to beliefs society holds, and others were beliefs more personal to you. Those that were false were corrected.

We are interested in discovering our beliefs—many being subconscious—because our own beliefs are the foundation for everything we do. We create what we think.

That doesn't always appear to be the case. "I didn't want to fail in my business," you say, "but I did." Or, "I work my fingers to the bone, and I still can't get ahead." You may even try affirmations that you repeat each morning, post on the car dash, or record to hear again and again. Yet, your experience isn't what you say you want.

The simple fact long recognized by educators, psychologists, and scientists is that our many subconscious beliefs supersede and overpower our conscious desires. That is their role. At some point we deem certain beliefs so important we give them an "automatic status." Whatever else we are to think, we decree that the certain beliefs we place into our subconscious will automatically guide our lives.

You put the beliefs into your subconscious mind, although the procedure isn't understood and you seldom know you're doing it. Many of these beliefs deal with the subject of wealth. For instance, if you experienced or perceived any kind of pain with wealth, or if you were taught that wealth was somehow unholy, bad, immoral, or corrupting, you may have programmed "I want to avoid any more money than I absolutely need." This belief, once programmed into your subconscious mind, will stay there until you clearly intend to remove it.

Sometimes the beliefs in our subconscious mind are beliefs from mass-consciousness—what everyone seems to believe. These beliefs are all around us. We hear them without even being aware of them. We intuitively know what they are, and they are so powerful that we opt to accept these without question. In computer language, they are our "default setting." We hold these beliefs without question, without examining their basis, without realizing they are there, and without knowing how they affect our lives.

In order to change that subconscious program you need to intend to change it. *INTEND* is the key.

Before you can intend to do anything, you have to know precisely what it is you do intend. It is very difficult to change a belief you've put into the subconscious until you know what that belief is, why you intend to replace it, and what new belief you intend to replace it with. That is why affirmations often fail. The false belief remains because you signaled no clear intention to remove it.

The procedure you're learning will reprogram your beliefs so they can be the foundation for abundance. On the first stroke you isolate your subconscious beliefs that are at odds with the natural laws of the cosmos. On the second stroke you learn a belief to accept into your subconscious that is in tune with natural law. Then you replace the false belief with the Truth.

Natural law provides for wealth and abundance for everyone. Anything less results from faulty thinking that inhibits the natural flow of wealth. When you have thoughts that allow you to accept the flow, money will come. It is just a matter of being in tune with the flow of nature's energy—the same energy that fires the sun, that transforms a seed into an oak tree, and that gives each of us the experience of being alive. You are created with all it takes to experience nature's energy to the fullest. Money and all other forms of abundance are aspects of that natural energy.

There is another type of thought that is a great inhibitor of wealth. In a way it is made up of thoughts that fall into the categories of the last two chapters. However, it is so insidious, so all-pervasive, and so debilitating that we must devote special time for it. I'm speaking of *fear*.

Feelings of fear come about when you don't perceive the whole picture. Fear requires some lack of knowledge. There is such perfect order in the universe that you could never be afraid if you knew everything. That idea may be contrary to your understanding.

Because of our limited perception, fear is sometimes inevitable. If we run into a lion on a mountain trail and death appears imminent, we would no doubt experience fear. However, if we knew how we fit into the whole scheme of life, what happens with and after death, what our role on earth is and why it may be coming to an end—if we indeed saw the whole picture, we couldn't be afraid.

That is not where most of us are at. We don't know everything. There are going to be times when we are frightened for seemingly good reasons, and we'll act as best we can. When a lion appears, we'll fight or flee and not take time to figure out the whole picture. I don't propose changing that response.

However, most of us do have some fears we can manage differently than we do. A general state of worry is one such fear that interferes with your ability to manifest wealth.

Worry thoughts are incredibly powerful. They carry such a wallop that too often you manifest what you are most afraid of. If you're worried you won't have enough money to pay your bills, chances are you won't. If you are worried you won't get a certain job, or promotion, or raise, you probably won't. If you are worried you're going to run out of money, you probably will. It is that simple, folks. If you dwell on something with enough worry, I guarantee you'll get something pretty close to it.

We're going to tackle two kinds of fear. First, we'll deal with the general condition of fear. Second, we'll tackle fear you associate with specific sets of circumstances. The techniques to come to grips with these fears will break down more walls separating you from your wealth.

Have you awakened at night worried? Or have you worn a frown all day? Often you'll justify your worry. You'll find something to focus on, but as soon as that gets resolved, you'll find something else to worry about.

This general worried state is quite crippling. It will surely affect your experiences, and might even help bring about what you are afraid of. As soon as possible you need to break out of it. Don't linger or wallow, because it is very powerful.

A simple technique can help you snap out of the worry state. The objective is to breathe fast and deep so you take in a lot of oxygen. The general state of worry has a physiological component that is transformed with deep breathing. Do whatever is comfortable to get your breath moving. Run or walk fast. Do pushups, sit-ups, or other kind of body exercise. You'll be amazed what it does for your frame of mind. Of course, use common sense, and don't push your body beyond comfortable limits. Always follow the advice of your physician when exercising.

Another technique to neutralize a general fear state is to lie down and breathe with the connected breaths you learned in Chapter Two. You can do this any time a fear feeling comes up. The deeper and faster the breathing, the better. If your legs or arms start to tingle or get numb, take slower and shallower breaths. When finished, breathe normally a couple of minutes before standing up.

Don't think for a moment I'm suggesting that you use breath instead of solving legitimate challenges. We all have projects that need attention. Often the challenges in life are baffling, but they are best met from a feeling of peace instead of fear.

Besides general states of worry and fear, you also need to come to grips with situations, circumstances, or conditions that scare you. These can sever your tie to money without your even knowing they exist.

For instance, if your parents always argued about money, you might have become afraid of talking about money. Or, perhaps you were doing quite well in a business venture that suddenly went sour. You lost all your money, and now you are afraid of business ventures.

These are the types of fears you need to identify. They are distinct from the beliefs and thoughts you dealt with in the last two chapters. These are feelings of fear that are associated with some set of circumstances. It is that set of circumstances you need to discover and address.

If you wrote down all the circumstances you thought gave you feelings of fear, you wouldn't make much progress. You would garner a list, but whether or not it would be accurate is open to conjecture. My guess is that it wouldn't be.

Instead, you can uncover your fear-associations by adapting the techniques that have brought you this far. Not surprisingly, I call this adaptation *Purging Fear-Associations.*

It begins with *The Basic Practice* for about ten minutes. Then think, "Give me a set of circumstances centering around money that gives rise to a feeling of fear." This technique can, of course, be used for any kind of fear, but we're focusing on wealth in this book. When you think you understand a set of circumstances, verify them with your "Yes" and "No" signals. Make a list in your journal of all the fear-associations you receive. Continue this process for about ten minutes and repeat the entire exercise for several sessions until you have identified all of your fear-associations. Like all these techniques dealing with the subconscious, finding all your fear-associations is an ongoing process. Repeat this periodically throughout life.

The next step is to erase the association. There is no single perfect method, so you can come up with your own way. At the end of the above session, ask, "What is the best procedure for me to erase these fears?" Listen to your thoughts for the procedure, and verify with your "Yes" and "No" signals. Then erase each fear-association, and write a description of your procedure in your journal.

Remember, by erasing, you only get rid of the debilitating nature of fear. You will not get rid of a positive concern that prompts you into some course of positive activity. You certainly want to retain that. It is only the fear-association that you erase.

By now I hardly need to remind you not to go on to the next chapter until you've uncovered and erased all of your fear-associations. With this accomplished, along with changing your personal thoughts and cleansing societal beliefs, you have a solid foundation to learn a practice for bringing a natural flow of wealth to you.

NEUTRALIZING FEAR-STATES

Technique One: Do whatever is comfortable to breathe fast and deep, such as running, walking, pushups, or sit-ups. Use common sense, and don't push your body beyond comfortable limits. Always follow the advice of your physician when exercising.

Technique Two: Lie down and breathe with connected breaths (no space between the in and out breaths) that are deep and fast. If your legs, arms, or face feel numb or tingle, take slower and shallower breaths. When finished, breathe normally a couple of minutes before standing up.

PURGING FEAR-ASSOCIATIONS

Step One: Ten minutes of The Basic Practice.

Step Two: Think, "Give me a set of circumstances centering around money that gives rise to a feeling of fear." The set of circumstances will come in your thoughts.

Step Three: Verify the set of circumstances with your "Yes" and "No" signals, and write it in your journal.

Step Four: Ask to be given a procedure to erase the fear-associations. It will come to you in your thoughts. Verify with your 'Yes" and "No" signals.

Step Five: Erase the fear-associations, and write a description of your procedure in your journal.

Chapter Seven

Empowerment

This completes the preparation for easy and direct flow of wealth.

You began the preparation by just observing the many different forms of vibration around you. From the simple awareness of rhythms in life, you moved on to *The Basic Practice,* which is nothing more than focusing on an aspect of your own cosmic vibration, your money rhythm. This might be a pulsation in the heart region that is not from the heart beat, or it might be a movement, a vision, or a sensation.

After you got *The Basic Practice* down pat, you learned the first tools for getting answers you need to know: "Yes" and "No" signals—another rhythm in the form of a movement, vision, or sensation that is pleasant and easily noticed.

With these new tools you were able to get to the heart of the preparation. In a true sense, it was house cleaning. You went into the attic of your subconscious mind where you store beliefs to throw out some, dust off others, and put in new ones. You did this by isolating your false beliefs that interfere with making money and correcting them. Then you isolated false beliefs that are part of mass-consciousness, and you corrected them. Finally, you learned what sets of circumstances cause feelings of fear so you could erase the fear-associations.

The cleansing you've just been through has left you with a foundation for power. Your beliefs are now your source for mighty empowerment.

Your power has always been there. Nothing has been added to the magnificent package you were created with. You've just done a little house cleaning. You just needed to tear away some of your false beliefs to expose the power you are. In that sense you learned nothing.

Your power comes from your thoughts. Nothing is done without an underlying thought. Some kind of mental activity must accompany every single act you do, even if the thoughts are subconscious. If you have a string of thoughts that doubt your worth, that belittle your capabilities, that are cynical about whether you can accomplish something, or that question every idea you have as unrealistic, you have no power. Anything you try—if you even try—is doomed for failure from the beginning.

Actually, to say you "have no power" is inaccurate. The power was always there, only it was misdirected. It was directed toward fulfilling the desires that arose from flawed thinking. Your new techniques introduce a set of empowering beliefs that are in tune with natural law, your true desires, and your role in life.

Instead of living at the mercy of false beliefs, you can govern your life with the power of Truth. If you don't like your experiences, you can now delve into the subconscious mind to find out what beliefs are giving you experiences you don't want. That deals with every aspect of life—your health, your marriage, friendships, work, recreation, prosperity, to name a few. You can improve every aspect of your life by cleaning out your "belief-chest" and packing it with thoughts that are the basis for new and better experiences.

The fact that thoughts are the basis of action is not a new notion. Sages for thousands of years have taught that. Modern psychology now respects the role of thoughts, even though there is disagreement on how to change them.

Thoughts are more than just impetus for activity. There is actually a link between our thoughts and the material world around us. That is why we spent so much time cleaning up your belief system.

When you say a belief out loud, it is vibration in the form of sound waves. That's obvious, but a thought is also a vibration. Indeed, everything that exists is some of vibration. Even solid metal is made up of vibrating sub-atomic particles.

Since the thought of an object and the object are both vibrations, is there be a link between them? Yes, there is. There is an actual vibrational linkage between what you think and what you get. Your thoughts attract, repel, and affect all the other vibrations around you. In a complicated interaction—far beyond present comprehension—your thoughts attract forces of nature to manifest in the physical world whatever you think.

Your mind is a giant transmitter that beams your thoughts to everyone and everything. Then quite miraculously, energy is mustered together to manifest what you think.

When nature is fully understood, we'll know we are bathing in a sea of consciousness made up of infinite rhythm and vibration, all interrelated and interdependent. What happens in one arena is felt in another. This isn't philosophy, or psychology, or metaphysics. This is simply the way the physical world is put together. There is nothing mysterious about it.

It isn't important that you understand this principle. Indeed, science is just beginning to grapple with the concepts. It is sufficient that you believe you are now ready to play confidently and successfully in this arena called life. All the forces of nature are your servants.

Because of the preparation you've just completed, you are now poised for action. Like an arrow pulled back on a bow, you only need to be aimed. How to aim is what you'll learn in the next section. There is nothing you can not accomplish. That is true empowerment.

Part II
The Practice

Chapter Eight

The Fundamental Habit

You are now prepared to learn how to get into the flow of wealth and stay with the flow. At least, you are prepared if you followed through on all your instructions to this point. If you just read Part I, don't move on. Go back and master each technique in order. These words by themselves make little sense. Only your experience can convey to you the meaning and Truth within these pages.

The purpose of this chapter is to develop *The Fundamental Habit* of a twice daily meditation-like practice. *The Fundamental Habit* is essential to get into the flow of wealth and to stay in the flow. It is the single most important thing you can do for self improvement.

The Fundamental Habit is two twenty minute sessions: one before breakfast and one before dinner. The first ten minutes or so is *The Basic Practice*, now an old hat for you. The remainder of the time is spent on correcting beliefs, purging fear, or practicing the new techniques you're going to learn. When all the techniques are mastered, the second ten minutes of *The Fundamental Habit* can be spent with any of them. The important point is that this is indeed to become a habit you will incorporate into your life. It doesn't end when all the techniques are mastered and you have finished this Course.

These sessions can be the most pleasant moments you spend each day. They are not a burden. They are a luxury you won't want to miss or give up. The more you do them, the more you'll look forward to these precious times.

A main characteristic of the practice is deep relaxation. The contrast is more noticeable in the evening session, but in the morning the deep relaxation is also present. Every muscle seems to go limp. Your head might droop. The shock of a phone ringing attests to how very quiet you are. This relaxation carries dividends beyond the enjoyment. It is the key to countless benefits.

A rested mind is more alert. A rested body is more responsive. Rest heals. Rest and relaxation melt away stress. Rest is the basis for peace of mind and a feeling of contentment. Indeed, rest is the basis for all your dynamic activity. If you did nothing except rest more and better, you would make more money and have a more fulfilling life.

Our bodies are programmed into cycles of rest and activity. Everything we do alternates between the two. We sleep each day. We blink our eye lids periodically. We even rest one foot while the other takes a step. The twice daily practice is a giant overlay for all our other rest/activity cycles.

After a few weeks of the practice, the deep relaxation will be expected by your body. If you miss a session, you might feel a longing for the rest it brings. A friend of mind started feeling tired a short time before her evening sessions. Even though the twenty minutes revitalized her, she was disturbed by the pattern. She viewed it as a weakness, I guess. One day she proudly announced she had weaned herself of the evening session. Such a shame! It is like having access to a Swiss bank account and throwing away the key. Don't buy into such nonsense.

Because your body will respond to these two periods by adapting its own cycle to them, it is best to do the sessions at approximately the same time each day. The body's reaction is similar for its sleep cycle. If you miss several hours of sleep or get to bed at a different time, your internal clock is disoriented.

Sometimes it won't be possible to do a session at the usual time. Instead of missing a session, opt for working it in when you can. It is better to change the time than not to do it at all—just like it is better to sleep at an unusual time than miss the sleep altogether.

Even your money rhythm is a variation of the rest and activity theme. All rhythms are. There is a period of movement or action, followed by quiet or silence. Then it repeats. All vibrations in the cosmos are made up of the same pattern: action, inaction, action, inaction, action, etc.

When an archer pulls back the string and stands still, he is poised for a thrust of activity. That is the inaction stage. Then he lets go and the arrow springs into action. Think of *The Fundamental Habit* as being like the moment the archer pulls the string. You're silent, but poised. When you come out of the session, you too spring into action.

That is why two daily periods are needed. Your night's sleep gives you a certain type of rest. *The Fundamental Habit* brings a deeper relaxation. From that twenty minutes you are ready to meet every challenge in the day. However, the day takes its toll. Some of your energy is drained, and you accumulate some stress. The evening session of deep relaxation dissolves that stress and infuses more energy. Because of *The Fundamental Habit*, your evenings are like a whole new day.

Relaxation is a real incentive to develop this habit, but there are more. Right away you feel on top of the world. You notice improvements in your health. Your mind is sharper. You feel peaceful, yet dynamic. Even bursts of happiness appear without apparent reason. These are real incentives to develop the habit, and they aren't imagined. Expect them.

Write in your journal a running account of all the improvements you notice. If you don't make note of them right away, they will be forgotten. Quickly the changes become part of your normal life, and you won't even remember how life was before *The Fundamental Habit*.

While improvements surely come into your life, they stay only as long as you keep up the practice. It's like the gym. You can't go there for two months, get into great shape, then quit. If you do, your gut reappears, and your muscles deflate. It is the same with *The Fundamental Habit*. The benefits from the deep relaxation will disappear if you stop the sessions. Of course, you will retain some residual improvements, but for the most part you will regress back to where you were.

Getting into the flow of wealth is the main reason you embarked on this adventure. Each time you sit with your money rhythm, that flow increases. It accumulates. However, if you wait a long time between sessions, you lose the momentum. The perfect practice for maximum benefit is twice daily for tw   enty minutes each. With that you increase the flow a bit each time. Keep this in mind. Regularity is key for maximum results.

If that's true, why not do more than two sessions each day? It doesn't help, and you may even experience some irritability or roughness. You are asking your nervous system to accommodate new vibrations—a new mode for your nervous system to operate in. It can only adapt slowly. Each time it accepts a little bit more of the cosmic vibration. Then for the next eight or nine hours the body makes whatever physical changes are required to carry the new vibration. Sometimes that means structural alterations for the nerves. Sometimes it means chemical variations. These changes are so minute they could never be monitored physically. However, they are reflected in your experiences—greater wealth, better health, more peace of mind, feelings of happiness, to mention a few. The proof of the pudding is in the eating. You're after a better life, and that's how you gauge your progress.

It might seem strange that your body plays a role in your abundance. Nevertheless, that is how basic this approach is. You have a technique that is actually changing your body to change your life experiences.

If you think about it, that shouldn't seem so strange. At the beginning of this Course you observed rhythms in your physical world. Then you zeroed in on your money rhythm. That too was physical. Maybe you got a nodding of your head, or a swaying of the back, or a movement of a finger. Maybe it was a pulsation someplace in your body. It was always physical. You saw it, felt it, or heard it. Your body was intricately involved.

The first experience of your money rhythm introduced it to your nervous system. Maybe it took several sessions before you actually noticed the rhythm. It wasn't because nothing was happening. Quite the contrary. Your nervous system was being asked to accommodate a new experience. It had to make changes. Nothing you could do would hurry up the process, except of course for repeated tries. Each time brought you closer, although you may have only felt frustration.

The same process continues. The rhythm probably seems the same to you now, although it may change from time to time also. Don't worry if it does—or doesn't. Each time you do *The Fundamental Habit,* you ask your nervous system to do just a little bit more. Of course, you aren't saying that, but your nervous system is aware of the tremendous vibration it wants to get in tune with. Automatically there are some physical adjustments at each session.

And what is that tremendous vibration the nervous system wants to get in tune with? It is nothing less than the flow of cosmic creative energy. It is the vibrating life of nature. You are made of it. Everything around you is made from it. It is available for your use to create wealth and abundance. The degree to which you are a creator with this energy would baffle the twentieth century intellect.

Regularly practiced, *The Fundamental Habit* brings you into harmony with the vibrations of the universe. These vibrations then submit to you while you submit to them. Total submission by both sides results in unlimited power and creativity.

These are the reasons you must develop a regular habit of two twenty minute sessions for *The Fundamental Habit.* This is on-going. You can't benefit from a single word in this book. Not one word has any magic.

The magic is solely your commitment to this practice. When you have made the commitment to be regular and have started, you can move on. In the following pages you receive more techniques to help bring wealth. *The Fundamental Habit*, however, is the most important element. With it, everything unfolds. Without it, life keeps on being a struggle.

The sign posts for your progress are the improvements to your life. Look for them. They are there.

In time—and it does take time—your nervous system will be ready to accommodate the vibrations of great wealth. Be patient. Have tenacity. The energy that is nature is waiting for you.

THE FUNDAMENTAL HABIT

Before breakfast and again before dinner do The Basic Practice for ten minutes. Devote another ten minutes to one of the other techniques from this Course.

Always end with each session a couple of minutes coming out slowly; not to do so may cause some irritability or roughness.

Set yourself up so as not to be disturbed. Always sit comfortably and close your eyes. It is okay to have thoughts, just slightly favor your money rhythm.

The subjective experience during the practice will vary from session to session. Don't be concerned about that. However, make a note in your journal of improvements in your everyday activities, such as more energy, better health, feelings of happiness, peace of mind, and greater income, to mention a few you can expect.

Regularity of this habit is key: twice a day for twenty minutes at approximately the same time each day.

Chapter Nine

Goal Setting

When we became adults, we barged into the money making world in many ways. Some of us went to trade schools or colleges, then interviewed at the placement office. Others fell into one career or another, almost by default, learning the basic skills on site. A few lucky ones stepped into family businesses.

Some of us float through life from job to job without a sense of purpose, plan, or goals. Others map out a strategy for attaining a set of achievements. A third group alternates back and forth between the two.

The second group is more creative, happier, and makes more money than either the floaters or the alternators. At work is the power of focus. When you focus, you are directing the creative vibrations of the cosmos. When directed, they manifest whatever you set out to create. That is natural law.

Right now I'm sitting in a formal garden at the home of one of San Diego's pioneers. The skies are deep blue, and the intense sun renews life all around me. Those sun rays are scattered. That is, they have no particular focus. Using a broken root beer bottle, I focus those sun rays onto a paper. In seconds the paper ignites. That is the power of focus.

Nature repeats herself. When something works, she uses infinite variations of the theme. The focus of the sun rays and the focus of our thoughts are two such variations of a natural law. The scattered sun rays can be focused to increase their power. Likewise, our scattered thoughts can be focused to increase their power. In both cases natural law provides for scattered and diffused energy to be concentrated and directed for greater power and creativity.

It might seem strange the same law of nature that is at work with sun rays is at work with our thoughts. Thoughts and sun rays seem totally different. They appear to have nothing in common. Yet they are both vibrations, and they are both expressions of creation's most elementary ingredient.

Albert Einstein touched on this in his research. We are just beginning to understand the implications of the laws of nature he defined. The most basic is his Unified Field Theory, which he intuitively knew to be true, although he died before he could prove it mathematically. What Einstein wanted to show is that everything in nature—everything everywhere—can be boiled down to a common and most elementary ingredient which he called The Unified Field.

Einstein came close. He could reduce creation to space, time, matter, energy, and gravitation. In his General Relativity, Einstein showed that space and time are a continuum. In his Special Relativity, he showed that matter and energy are the same. Gravity appeared to stand alone. Einstein wanted to show The Unified Field is more elementary than space, time, matter, energy, and gravitation, and it unifies all five. The Unified Field, he felt, is the basis of everything else.

Einstein was right. Science is on the verge of proving his theory. The Unified Field does exist, and it is no more than a particular kind of vibration which underlies all the cosmos. It is the life force of living creatures, and it is the energy of the inanimate worlds as well. It is the power and energy behind the scenes. In a nutshell, it is the creative power of the universe.

The Unified Field created the big bang. It brought about the variety of forms and life on earth, not to mention the forms and life we can't comprehend millions of light years away. It is intelligence. It is order.

It is perfection. It is nature. It is infinite power, as well as ultimate silence. All that is, or can be imagined, is a variation arising from The Unified Field.

Every conceivable expression of that basic vibration, The Unified Field, could exist someplace in the cosmos. Simply the focus and direction of this elementary energy could manifest anything. And it does. All the time.

Einstein's Unified Field Theory is very important for us to appreciate. We don't need to know the physics formula. We don't need to figure out if his theory belongs to the science of mathematics or the science of physics. We don't need to trace that elementary vibration to space, or time, or energy, or matter, or gravitation. We don't have to find the Unified Field in plants, or in animals, or in our bodies, or even in our souls. No. We don't have to understand any of that. It works for us without depth of understanding. However, it won't work for us without a focused connection.

Your money rhythm is that focused connection. By sitting twenty minutes twice a day for *The Fundamental Habit*, you open up yourself to the most elementary vibrations of the cosmos. The Unified Field and all it represents becomes yours for the asking.

This is not particularly profound. This is actually the way creation is put together. We were created with that link to our most basic nature. Awareness of our most basic nature is also awareness of creation's most basic nature. To have that awareness is natural, and that is what you are learning to do.

Your thoughts are part of The Unified Field. After all, if The Unified Field underlies everything, that means EVERYTHING. We don't think of thoughts as being something, but they are. They have an existence in time. They are a form of vibration. Isn't that all anything really is? Everything is a vibration in time, including our thoughts.

Since thoughts are an aspect of nature's most elementary vibration, thoughts are a direct outgrowth of the same energy that made the lily, the peacock, and the quartz crystal. Thoughts are a direct outgrowth of creative intelligence and much more than just fleeting images in someone's brain.

Deeply embedded in each thought is its access to The Unified Field, its link to creative intelligence, and its ability to create what it represents. That is the scheme of nature. Everything in creation is tied together, and we are part of that unity. We are also proof of its diversity. Unity in diversity. Diversity in unity.

Thoughts touch the silent vibration of The Unified Field, and it is through thoughts that we give direction to the vast sea of intelligence around us. Thoughts give focus to creative energies.

To acknowledge this very basic nature of your thoughts is to empower them. You don't even have to understand it. Acknowledgement is enough. How grateful the artist is when someone appreciates his painting. The person doesn't need to know how he got the special effect, why certain colors were chosen, or what brushes were used. Just the appreciation opens the artist's heart. Nature is the same way. Appreciate the incredible link with everything, and nature's heart opens up to you. Everything nature has is yours for the asking. FOR THE ASKING! Remember that: for the asking. That is the role of our thoughts. We just need to think. Our thoughts carry the power to manifest what they contain.

Since your thoughts are so powerful, you have to be careful what you think. They were powerful enough before you started this book. Now you've added a jolt of power to your thoughts by taking your awareness to a fundamental vibration. From now on, be very, very careful what you think. Your thoughts manifest.

Even your seemingly idle thoughts manifest. Don't joke, "I'm on the way to the poor-house." It has its effect. Clean up all your expressions. Say and think only what you truly want. Carefully monitor every utterance. You will find many of your words you really do not mean. You would be horrified if they came true. Carefully monitor!

You also need to set goals to give your thoughts direction. Every person in the flow of wealth has goals. A white water rafter might be letting the current carry him, but he has a goal. He isn't being knocked around the river without a destination. He knows where he is going. He may not know how he'll tackle each rapid, but he knows his destination and his goal.

Goal setting is not new. Every course I've seen on money making starts out with a goal setting section. They make you decide right away, once and for all, exactly what you want to accomplish this year, in five years, and maybe in your life. WOW!! Now, that's scary, but people grope and struggle to come up with answers. They have little experience and miniscule intelligence as their guide.

Well, by now you know that isn't the way you'll set your goals. You can't know from your limited experience and conscious knowledge what your highest and wisest goals are. No matter how long you contemplate, or how hard you rack your brain, you can't know the answer from that level of your thinking.

There is an inner-most aspect of you that can give the answer. It is reliable, and it sets your ship of fate in the perfect direction. To tap that inner-most resource, you use the tools you're now quite familiar with.

For the next few days in the second ten minutes of *The Fundamental Habit*, ask, "What are my highest and wisest goals for five years from now." The answer will come in your thoughts. Verify with the help of your "Yes" and "No" signals. Then, make a list of these goals in your journal, and incorporate them into your overall outlook and thinking.

After all the five years goals are complete, ask "What are my highest and wisest goals for the next year?" Again, put them in your journal and incorporate them into your outlook and thoughts.

The third question is equally important. It sets the tone for your life. Ask, "What are my highest and wisest goals for my life?" Put those life goals in your journal. Let them guide everything you do.

It may take several days to do this. Be in no hurry.

Keep in mind that everything you will ever learn from these techniques is only for the present time. So, any goals you come up with are goals to hold for the present moment, for the now. It is the present thought of the goals that is important. It catapults you to new heights. Don't be surprised if the goals change as you advance. Goals do change as we change. Be willing to let that happen. For that reason, check your goals periodically throughout life to see if they need to be modified. A rafter must be prepared to change goals when the river current demands it.

Perhaps for the first time in your life, you can have a picture of what your life is all about. The answer to the question "Why am I here?" need not escape you any longer.

DISCOVERING YOUR GOALS

STEP ONE: Begin with the first ten minutes of The Fundamental Habit.

STEP TWO: Ask, "What are my highest and wisest goals for five years from now?" Use your "Yes" and "No" signals to help verify the goals that come in your thoughts. Write down these five year goals in your journal.

STEP THREE: Use the same procedure to find out your highest and wisest goals for one year from now. Write them in your journal.

STEP FOUR: Use the same procedure to find out your highest and wisest goals for your life? Write these life goals in your journal.

Check all of these goals periodically to see if they need to be modified. As you evolve in life, your goals may need some changes. They are not etched into stone by this exercise.

The entire time for each session is about twenty minutes.

Chapter Ten

A Plan of Action

You could not learn your goals by asking someone else what your goals ought to be. Not even your parents, spouse, or best friend can tell you. Your goals are as personal as your finger prints. A problem arises because everyone around has their own ideas about what your life should be. They often make a point of hammering it in. "You know what you should do...?" "If I were you, I'd..." "When are you going to get your act together?"

This comes from meaningful people. They honestly have your best interests in their hearts. The simple fact is that none of them can know what your goals might be. None of them. Nature has a privacy doctrine, and no one is privy to your inner-most thoughts, desires, and purpose. Only you can tap into that.

So-called psychics can not invade your privacy either, except occasionally with your express permission. Even then it is so limited that it can not be trusted.

Discovery of your goals is totally on your shoulders. That is a real challenge to do without outside influence. You may have tried coming up with a list before you learned the last technique. Surely one or two items were what your father wants for you. Or your uncle's emphasis in life might have crept in. Or you might have been overly concerned about the welfare of someone you support. Your intellect is keenly aware of other people and their values, but your true goals must transcend all of that.

Think of your life like a trip. When you boarded this adventure you packed several bags filled with all you would need—your talents, your qualities, your weaknesses, your strong points, your aptitude, your family wealth and status, and your physical stamina, to mention a few. You packed up and brought whatever you need to be comfortable on this journey and to do all the things you want to do. You forgot what you brought, but inside the bags you have a list of everything. Only you—and no one else— knows what is on the list.

If no one else knows what you brought into this life, how could anyone possibly tell what you should do? No one can. You knew when you came what you want to accomplish, and you brought with you everything you need to accomplish it.

This implies you have more than you brought. Indeed. You are made of The Unified Field—that basic building block for all of creation. Within that building block resides all the intelligence, power, qualities, and diversity of creation. That means within you reside the infinite variety of the cosmos. Yet you brought into this life only what you need to do your work.

The first clue to discover your highest and wisest goals is what you brought into this life. If you have tremendous talent for singing, maybe a goal would involve music. If you could scarcely carry a tune, it would be senseless to try to become an opera singer in five years. Yet how many parents try to steer children in such foreign directions?

All the goals you formulated in the last chapter are attainable. You have all the innate talents and qualities to be successful. More than likely, you are looking forward to diving in. It will be fun, and it will be easy.

Goals can be on every facet of life. Your goals may have included something on health, or relationships, or education, as well as the goal for this Course: Money Making. Whatever the issue, the process is the same. For money making, your goal might be to earn a certain income. Or the goal might be to have your own store, or to become promoted to vice president at work, or to have all your bills cleared up.

The money related goals you came up with are where you want to be at some future time. Now you need plans of action to fulfill the goals. It is fine and dandy—indeed necessary—to have ultimate goals, but they are empty without plans of action.

The blueprints to your dream home are only a necessary first step. You'll need to get the down payment together, to find the financing, to find the perfect location, to find a contractor, and so on. Each step requires some form of action by you.

At each step along the way you have many options. Each decision leads you to another set of options. And so it goes until your goal is met.

It is obvious that some avenues to your goal will be swift, while other avenues are slow. Some avenues will expose you to new adventures and learning, while others chart only a familiar course. Your conscious intellect does not know which path really serves your highest and wisest interest.

When you think about it, you don't even know why a particular goal is best for you. For instance, is your goal of becoming vice president at work to get a higher income so you can send your children to college? Or is the goal to give you the experience of rising up the corporate ladder? The reason would certainly affect your choice of options.

Why do you think a particular money goal is on your list? I would bet a thousand dollars to a donut you may not be certain of the reason. If you aren't certain why a goal is on your list, how can you wisely choose a path to its fulfillment? You can't. None of us can.

We guess, and we flounder. Inner-guidance does speak. Some hear it better than others. Usually we're listening to chatter in our heads from five stations at once, so the inner-guidance is hardly distinguishable. We're lucky if the guidance even gets weighed as an option.

Your next assignment is to discover an initial set of options in your plan of action to meet each of your money related goals.

Your inner-intelligence calculates a perfect plan of action as soon as you set a goal. That is automatic. As soon as you decide what you want, your "on-board computer" knows exactly how to realize the goal, taking everything into account. It considers your talents, qualities, education, weaknesses, stamina, resources and reason for the goal to come up with a viable plan of action. This happens for everyone all the time. This is nothing new. What is new is to realize it happens and then to retrieve the information.

Furthermore, with every little modification you make in your goal, that inner-intelligence spontaneously alters the path to incorporate the changes. At all times there is a complete plan of action that is perfect for you to realize your goals.

For instance, take a goal to become vice president at work. Your inner intelligence would know if that is a goal so you can make more money to send your children to college, or if the goal is to give you experience in rising up the corporate ladder. Knowing the reason, your mind will calculate the perfect path and most appropriate options for maximum benefit to you.

Moreover, your mind is directly linked via The Unified Field to everything around you. It knows all the outside resources at your disposal and incorporates the available people and materials to be drawn to you like a magnet. Never included are resources that are in short supply, or that would be frustrating, or uncooperative. With the mind's plan of action you flow with the resources to reach your goal easily, taking into account the reason for the goal.

At the same time the people you're working with are realizing their goals. It is like a group of people rafting down the river together. They each reach their goal, and they each help each other. They flow with minimum effort, carried mostly by the momentum of nature. When you are truly in tune with your plans of action, and when all the people around you are in tune with their plans, everyone benefits. Then life is fun. Everyone helps everyone else without even trying.

In your assignment I purposely said *initial* plan of action instead of *complete* plan. You only want to find out your first set of options. This is contrary to the teachings of most courses on money making. They usually have you come up with a detailed plan from beginning to end. That is not going to be our approach.

Without compromising determination, your approach is to be more flexible. That requires moving in smaller increments, beginning with the first step. Chances are you won't be given only one possible action. Instead you'll need to choose one from among many equally appropriate options. Then do the activity required in your choice and uncover the next set of options.

Sometimes the experiences along the path are the more significant than the goal itself. By keeping yourself flexible for changes and new options, you'll reach your goal with maximum benefit and growth.

The option you choose and the way you tackle it will affect the options of the next step. Taking all that into consideration, your mind automatically calculates the subsequent courses of action. It is like the word processor I'm using to write this. I just decided to add a word in the previous paragraph. As each letter was added, the entire paragraph readjusted to the change. At any point, all the words lined up, the spacing was correct, and the paragraph looked complete.

In the same way your mind—your "on-board computer"—calculates to adjust your path for each step completed or for any change whatsoever. At any moment, the goal and its path is clear in your mind.

I've had students rebel with this approach until they experienced that they were in fact using their own tools. At first they thought they were giving up their power. They wanted to decide their own plan. They wanted to be totally in charge, and they perceived this approach was giving up power to someone or something else.

Let's get this straight right now. No one else—in or out of a body—is dictating your plan of action. The tools are your tools, and they expose your goals and your plans. Not to discover them is to waste your potential.

Rather than giving up your power, you are actually reclaiming your power. That is empowerment. I keep harping on the concept of empowerment because that is what this is. With power you can flow from step to step and realize all your goals.

By now, you don't need to be told how to discover the initial step in your plan of action for your money related goals. The procedure is all too familiar.

During the second ten minutes of *The Fundamental Habit*, ask, "What are my initial options for reaching my goal of (state the goal)?" Listen for the answer in your thoughts. Verify it with your "Yes" and "No" signals.

Do this for each of the goals on your list and write the answers in your journal. Set aside a page or two for each goal so all the steps can be written down together as they unfold.

Choose one of the options and do the action called for. Then use the same procedure to discover the next set of options. Continue without doubting, without judgment, and without anticipation. Step by step you'll go to your goal in the most direct path for maximum growth and rewards. All your strengths will be used. All your weaknesses will be bypassed. All the resources around you will be summoned to your aid. There is within you a perfect plan of action for every goal. Go with it.

DISCOVERING YOUR PLANS OF ACTION

STEP ONE: Begin with the first ten minutes of The Fundamental Habit.

STEP TWO: *During the second ten minutes, ask, "What are my initial (or next) options for reaching my goal of (state the goal)?" Listen for the answer in your thoughts. Verify with the aid of your "Yes" and "No" signals.*

Discover only one step at a time. Choose an option and do the action. Then repeat the process for the next step. Continue in this manner until the goal is reached.

Do this for each of the goals on your list and write the steps in your journal. Set aside a page or two for each goal so all the steps can be written down together as they unfold.

Do not anticipate, judge, or doubt. Be flexible, knowing the process will take you the most direct route, all factors considered.

Chapter Eleven

Managing the Flow

The white water rafter has a goal and a plan of action. He doesn't head into the rapids blindly. He has a safe boat and a rudder, but he allows the natural flow of the water to take him to his goal.

It is just that simple for your goals as well. The almighty power of nature is your propellant. You decide your goals, you make the choices, and you delve into activity. It is the endless energy of creation that guides and carries you to fulfilling your goals.

You don't blindly follow. It is not an aimless experience. We see people all the time who profess to be flowing, and we want nothing of what they're doing. They seem to lead a lazy, shiftless lives without much purpose. They flounder from job to job. They eat from hand to mouth. That kind of flowing is like a boat without a rudder. It gets tossed around in the current, and anyone taking that ride is apt to get sick.

It is one thing to aimlessly submit to the pressures and forces around you and quite another thing to flow with nature with goals and with a plan of action. Don't abdicate your rightful throne. Don't lose your free-will. Instead, be empowered with all the forces of nature at your command. The king has all the resources of his kingdom, and he knows how to muster them. You are royalty, and now you know how to muster the resources of your kingdom.

The kind of flowing you're doing is powerful in part because of its efficiency. A skilled oarsman knows precisely the stroke needed for each maneuver. He would loose momentum and time if he had to experiment along the way. His skill assures him of victory. The oarsman wastes no motions, he loses no energy, and he gets maximum speed from his boat. So it can be for you. You can be skilled in all your actions. Quite spontaneously, you can go from step to step, wasting not a single breath, not a single step, not a single moment, not a single movement.

Remember the race between the turtle and the hare? Each step the turtle made was a correct step in the right direction. He used his own resources for maximum efficiency. To the contrary, the rabbit wasted time, he ran all over the place, and he didn't focus on the goal. To any observer it would seem that the rabbit was doing so much more than the turtle. He was far more active. He exerted far more energy. Still, he lost.

It is all a matter of efficiency. Efficiency means skill in your action. It means you can accomplish more yet do less.

Flowing with nature is not coping out. Flowing with nature is knowing how to become efficient. You do this by first coming up with the perfect goals for yourself. These goals reflect your bag of talents, training, aptitude, and resources. It just wouldn't make sense to take on a goal you were ill-prepared to achieve.

Next, you discover the steps that lead to fulfillment of the goal. You have to work; there's no room for laziness. You have choices; you can't abdicate responsibility. All the work you do and any decisions you make lead you to success. It is the most efficient system you could devise.

When you flow with such efficiency, you have the time and the energy to take on twice or three times the projects. What a dynamo you'll be. Everyone will wonder where you get the energy and time to accomplish so much. Feel free to share your secret with others. Your example is their greatest teacher.

When your flowing really gets going and you are very busy with all your projects, you may be tempted to postpone or forget *The*

Fundamental Habit. Don't. That habit is the motor of your success. Each time you experience the deep relaxation with your money rhythm, you are recharging your batteries. After a few hours, they tend to fade. The twice daily infusion is necessary to maintain peek performance.

I know people who stop their twenty minute sessions when they get busy. That is tragic. Time and energy is wasted, and they miss their mark. Whatever they think they lose by investing twenty minutes is made up many times with increased efficiency.

Flowing is quite dynamic, and it requires all that you have to give. This flowing uses every ounce of your talent and training, but it does not ever require something you can't do. The turtle used all he had, and he wasn't required to run like the rabbit to win. That is the beauty of flowing.

Remember the flower analogy in Chapter One? To flow with nature is to flower. After all, flowing with nature is what causes a flower. If the rose bush weren't flowing with nature, there couldn't be a single bud.

There is nothing that impedes your flow with nature more than anger. It is tantamount to the white water rafter dragging an anchor. It makes the boat difficult to steer. Forward progress is nearly impossible. The boat might even capsize. To drag an anchor is downright dangerous.

Anger is also downright dangerous. You know that. You've experienced it. Anger only makes matters worse because it cuts you off from the flow. There is no way you could learn your goals or your plan of action under the influence of anger. Hell would freeze over first.

So, in order to manage the flow, you must develop a way to manage anger. This does not mean you never feel angry. There are times when you must make a point. You must rise to meet an occasion. Being forceful, even temporarily angry, may be the only way to get a point across. Jesus becoming outraged with the vendors in the temple is an example. He needed to make a point—and he did!

Those times are rare. Don't rationalize senseless angry fits as being necessary. They can destroy you. Anger cuts you off from the flow and from your quest for wealth.

You can neutralize anger with these four words: Love, Heart, Give, and Receive.

From them make four sentences:

> I give you my love;
> I give you my heart;
> I receive your love;
> I receive your heart.

Then whenever you feel angry, look at or visualize the person that perturbs you and think the four sentences until the anger subsides.

The anger goes. At least it mellows out. Energy from those sentences is broadcast into the atmosphere. Although the person you're angry with won't hear the words, he or she responds to the loving energy. The edge is immediately cut and a semblance of reason returns.

Those words are also good for the slow festering kind of anger. Because our thoughts touch The Unified Field, they pierce time and space. Problems from the past can be healed with the sentences. Even rifts with people thousands of miles away or deceased can be cleared up. These words are truly precious, and they should become a regular part of your flow management.

You don't have to resolve the issue that made you angry before you think the four sentences. The issue and the feelings of anger are two separate things. Do resolve the issue in time, but it can't be resolved while you're still angry.

These four sentences will help erase the feelings of anger so you can keep flowing. Once the angry feelings are gone, you can discover the first step toward a plan of action to unravel the conflict. Do resolve the problem. Otherwise you just might invite another fit of anger.

Stay on top of all the situations that might make you angry. When you come to grips with them early, your flow is hardly interrupted.

Without dealing with them, they will create more problems and of course more anger.

One rock lodged in a pipe can cause many other rocks to lodge. Before you know it, water stops flowing through the pipe. In the same way, anger builds up to stop your flow.

I've run into people who think they perform best when they are angry, that it is a driving force. That is nonsense. With anger at your helm, you are driving without true goals and without a step-by-step plan of action.

Expert management of your life can be easy now. Practice The Fundamental Habit regularly, and come to grips with anger. Discover your goals and the steps to fulfill them. The management of the flow is then automatic.

RELIEVING ANGER

Whenever you feel angry, visualize or see the person that prompted the anger and think these four sentences:

> *I give you my love;*
> *I give you my heart;*
> *I receive your love;*
> *I receive you heart.*

These sentences can be thought for situations that happened recently or a long time ago. They work regardless of whether or not the person you're angry with is present, thousands of miles away, or even deceased.

Repeat the sentences as many times as needed to get rid of the feelings of anger.

Chapter Twelve

Forgiveness

The lingering feelings we get when we think someone has hurt us is similar to anger. Perhaps something is said. Perhaps your body is injured. Or perhaps something you own is damaged or taken. No one is immune from this experience and the lingering feelings.

Our first reaction is anger, and it can be dissipated with those four precious sentences: I give you my love; I give you my heart; I receive your love; I receive your heart. This helps the anger, but often there remains a deeply rooted hurt or feeling of injustice. Left to fester, it surely interferes with our flow of wealth.

The remedy is simply forgiveness, although most of us would resist forgiving. An apology is what we think we want.

Forgiveness to heal those deeply rooted wounds might seem inappropriate because forgiveness is not understood. We were taught to forgive by saying something like this to the person: "You have done a terrible thing to me, but I am going to try to forget it and forgive you." This is certainly better than nothing, but you rehash the incident and focus your energies on the painful feelings. Such an approach to forgiveness often does little more than bring the awful incident to the surface again. The hurt continues to fester.

The festering of a grudge is actually the denial of your power and your flow with nature. You are thinking that someone can interfere with you to such a degree your rightful dues are taken and that you are powerless to stop it. That is an illusion.

Remember, the flow is actually the flow of The Unified Field. It is the flow of the building block of creation. The flow represents all of creation, and just by being in the flow, we touch each and every aspect of creation. That is why abundance and wealth come to us when we are flowing.

There is nothing in creation that can't flow to us from The Unified Field, and that flow is part of each of us naturally. Only a denial of the flow can stop its effects. We can't ever separate ourselves from The Unified Field, but we can turn down its gifts by not accepting it as our nature.

When you hold a grudge, essentially you are denying your connection to creation. You somehow think that you can be made a lesser person, or that your wealth can be taken away, or even that someone can do irreparable harm to you. All those things are impossible. You have as part of your basic nature all you need to be whole. You have that because you are made of the ingredient that makes everything.

If someone steals from you, or if your property is damaged, you can easily replenish it—provided you are in the flow. If someone hurts your body, miracles can heal it—provided you are in the flow. If someone belittles you, the knowledge of who you are and what your potential is casts off the remarks like water on a duck's back—provided you are in the flow.

Unresolved grudges deny who you are. They seem to give truth to your limitations and vulnerability. Then by your invitation, the flow appears to be cut off.

Since the flow can't actually stop, what is happening? Well, the flow is simply creating what you're expecting. When you think you can be irreparably injured, that is what manifests. When you think someone can take away your abundance, or a part of it, that is what manifests. Your thoughts and your intentions control The Unified Field that is within you. Your thoughts and intentions are the driving force for your world to manifest around you. Think grudge, then lack or injury will be your experience. Think that you can't be hurt, and that will be your experience.

So you see, grudges are a denial of your Self. They deny your basic nature. They invite suffering, poverty, and injustice. These are all illusions, but appear as very concrete realities. Grudges cause a cycle of illusions. To break those cycles, you must learn to forgive in a way that renews your experience of the flow.

The first step in forgiveness is to find the silver lining. It is always there.

On a camping trip on Maui my rental car was vandalized. A window was smashed, and the battery was stolen. Being in a remote area compounded the problem. A day was lost getting to a telephone, meeting the police, and getting a replacement car. I was upset and disillusioned about the safety of my chosen camp, so I drove to another. That evening I became friends with a musician. Six months later he composed and recorded two perfect piano and flute pieces for my workshops.

I could dwell on the injustice of the vandalism. Or I could see a rosy side. The music that is so important to me now came only because I met the musician. That never would have happened without moving camps because of the vandals. In a strange sense, I am grateful to them. The trauma did have a silver lining.

Everything that happens to you can be linked to something positive. Everything. You do need to search for it, and you do need to expect something. When you find out how your life has been changed because of a difficult incident, you can be grateful.

Sometimes the silver lining is just an opportunity for learning something. When I practiced law, I did more than my share of divorces. Invariably my clients felt rejected, abandoned, and hurt. Yet I saw for those willing to tackle the challenge, a "coming out." They gained self sufficiency and power.

I guess most of my clients never felt grateful to their estranged spouse for that growth. Instead, most continued to harbor ill-feelings and bitterness. Those feelings became monkeys on their backs to create more problems in their lives. They needed to begin the process of forgiveness by first seeing the silver lining and feeling grateful.

The opportunity for growth is enormous even in physical handicaps. What a tragedy it must be to lose one's sight. Indeed it is, but there must be a silver lining, even here. Ask Helen Keller. She is one person who perceives a silver lining for being both blind and deaf. That gave her an inner awareness that would have been more difficult to achieve with a sighted focus on the outer environment.

To lose one's sight evokes all our sympathy. It sings of unjustified tragedy. I use that example, because in all circumstances we must look for a silver lining. Not to do so enslaves us to pity and pain. Finding it opens the heart to the wonders of life.

Sometimes the silver lining is the development of powers you have but don't use until necessary. This can include becoming more intuitive or even clairvoyant. You might be steered toward developing talents or embarking on a different career. New people might come into your life. The silver lining can come in any form. One thing is certain: it will be there if you look hard enough.

How often have you had to be very depressed before you had the guts and incentive to pull yourself up? Sometimes a certain snide remark is just the catalyst for change, or at least realizing a problem.

I've had automobile accident clients who weren't expected to live. They mustered all the will they could and pulled themselves up. Their dilemma enlivened their will-power. It became the backbone for the rest of a dynamic life.

Of course, you can't come to grips with debilitating grudges until you identify them. Many have been forgotten, but they still interfere in your life. They're lodged in the subconscious, so you can't just make a list. It would be woefully incomplete.

To discover your grudges, use *The Fundamental Habit*. During the second ten minutes ask, "What grudges do I hold that I need to forgive?"

When an incident for which you're still harboring a grudge appears in your thoughts, ask, "How did that situation benefit me?" Verify the answer you get with your "Yes" and "No" signals.

Continue for as many sessions as you need to discover all your grudges. Keep track of each grudge and its silver lining in your journal.

Simply knowing the grudges in light of their silver linings lifts the clouds. It makes *The Act Of Forgiveness* easy. To forgive, merely think the essence of a basic Truth: life is for giving love. Look at that Truth carefully. Life is FOR GIVING love. "For giving." "Forgiving." Forgiveness is simply giving love.

That is all there is to forgiveness. You just need to give love. Our four precious sentences work perfectly here. Visualize the person and think with a sense of gratitude for the silver lining: "I give you my love; I give you my heart; I receive your love; I receive your heart." That's it. You need not forget the incident. You need not confront the person. You just give love in your thoughts, and the act of forgiveness is complete. It opens up the flow of creativity, abundance, wealth, and money.

DISCOVERING GRUDGES AND SILVER LININGS

STEP ONE: Begin with the first ten minutes of The Fundamental Habit.
STEP TWO: Ask, "What grudges do I hold that I need to forgive?" A situation will come to you in your thoughts. Verify with your "Yes" and "No" signals.
STEP THREE: Ask, "How did that situation benefit me?" Wait for the dawning thought to arise, then verify it with your "Yes" and "No" signals.
Continue the questions for about ten minutes.

THE ACT OF FORGIVENESS

Think of the situation and the people involved with a sense of gratitude for the silver lining. When that is firmly in your mind, think: "I give you my love; I give you my heart; I receive your love; I receive your heart."

There is no need to forget about the incident. There is no need to confront the people. Just give love in your thoughts.

Chapter Thirteen

Manifesting Your True Desires

The practice is almost complete. You are now locked into the flow with *The Fundamental Habit* twice a day. You have identified your goals, and you know how to accomplish them step by step.

The process requires no reasoning, conjecturing, or cogitating. This is all very good, but you have a reasoning intellect, and the flowing concept is foreign to it. Your intellect views this approach with skepticism. After all, it goes against the grain of everything you've been taught in school.

From our earliest days, we were trained from Sesame Street through college to think, think, think. Make a mistake, and we heard, "Use your head!" To decide on a career, we were told to weigh all our options and then make an intelligent decision. We are even surrounded by toys for our intellect: computers, books, paper, and manuals.

We are taught the only way to get answers is to learn, read, research, reason, deduce, and test. All of this is done with our intellect. It has become king, and it claims to be our almighty power. If we have a keen intellect that is well educated, then we are told we are on the road to success.

Educating the intellect is indeed necessary—probably essential—to meet many of your goals. Your intellect grasps your situation and your environment to give you perspective. To do that, it needs to be well-informed. At the same time you must realize it is not the only source for your power and success.

I've observed that most of the people that are attracted to this Course are the educated. Those people seem to feel there is much more out there at their disposal, and they want to find it. The problem arises when they barge in. Then the intellect with all its training questions and doubts, while the intuition tries to answer. An internal dialogue between the two voices ensues.

The intellect tries to tell you this is silly, dumb, and a pipe dream. Your intuition answers that it seems comfortable and worth a try. So, the intellect tells you it might be dangerous—you might get wacky. The intuition feels it is safe. And so it goes.

There is truly a danger in this banter: the intellect can get you to quit the practice before you discover its fruits. How sad that would be. You would be left with only what your intellect has to offer, which is what you have learned and not forgotten. That would be your sole source of your power. Most of nature's energy would be missed, even though it is you, it is all around you, and it is within you.

One effective way to deal with the intellect is to give it a role in the practice. After all, the conflict arises when we set the intellect aside and pretend it isn't needed any longer. Like a neglected child, it throws a tantrum.

Now we have reached a point where your intellect has a role to play. It is going to be in charge of *The Mind Treatment*, and it is an important role. Mind treatments are very powerful and a necessary ingredient in your quest for wealth. They are a guide for what and how to think to manifest specific goals.

All through this Course the power of your thoughts has been a reverberating theme. Every step has somehow involved correcting or refining your thinking. *The Mind Treatment* adds another layer to that refinement.

What you manifest with the intellect is limited to what it knows—limited to the quality and accuracy of the knowledge it has accumulated. Intuition, on the other hand, is unlimited. It can tap any knowledge anywhere in creation because it operates at the level of The Unified Field.

The Mind Treatment requires both the intellect and the intuition. Your intuition taps universal knowledge, and the intellect pulls together the five steps in the formula.

Begin with ten minutes of *The Fundamental Habit*. Then with the money rhythm in your awareness, go through the five steps of *The Mind Treatment*.

In the first step think of some of the qualities you share with nature. Preface each quality with "I am."

For example, you might think, "I am abundance. I am always seeking balance. I am perfect. I am always healing any injuries. I am intelligent. I am from The Unified Field. I am a part of a greater wholeness. I am at peace. I am infinite energy."

These are openers. Come up with some more of your own. The possibilities are endless because you are acknowledging the attributes of an infinite cosmos to which you belong.

The second step is to state clearly in the present tense what it is you want. However, before actually stating it, use your "Yes" and "No" signals to verify the desire is in your highest and wisest interest. It can be one of your goals. It can be one of the steps to a goal. Or it can be something specific you haven't addressed as part of a goal yet.

To state your desire, use the words "I manifest...." For instance, you could say, "I manifest the job at Sears, or better." Always use the words "or better" whenever you can to be open for something more appropriate. Indeed, if it is more appropriate, you would truly rather have it.

You may manifest in general terms, such as happiness, love, abundance, perfect health, enjoyment, fun, intelligence, guidance, peace of mind, and so on. These are simply statements of your general entitlements. *The Mind Treatment* for such matters is powerful, and it helps you to stay in the flow for a continuous experience of abundance and a well balanced life.

You may also manifest for something more specific, but always include "or better" where appropriate. "I manifest an income of $100,000 a year, or better." "I manifest the perfect publisher for my book on natural health." "I manifest a new BMW, or better."

It is very important you believe you can accomplish what you said you want. If the statement is so grand you don't believe it, then your disbelief will be the dominant thought. Use a goal that is clearly achievable.

The third step is to heal and release any false beliefs that might keep you from having what you want. This is old hat. You've done this several times now, from different angles. This is just a new slant. Ask, "Do I have any false beliefs that could keep me from manifesting this true desire?" With the aid of your "Yes" and "No" signals, find out what they are.

For each false belief you discover, find out the Truth to replace it. Devise an instant ritual to heal and release the false belief and to replace it with the Truth. For instance, you might visualize burning the false belief and watching the Truth arise from the ashes. Or, you might want to write down the false belief, violently cross it out or tear it up, and write down the Truth. Whatever seems comfortable to you is fine. Your intention is the key.

The fourth step is to forgive where needed. A grudge can stand in the way of whatever you want. Simply find out if anyone needs to be forgiven, using the "Yes" and "No" signals as an aid. For each person think your four familiar sentences: "I give you my love; I give you my heart; I receive your love; I receive you heart."

The fifth step is to accept with gratitude what you stated you want. It comes to you from almighty nature of which you are a part. It comes to you because you are created to experience all aspects of the cosmos. That is true abundance. Be grateful and allow the abundance to flow to you.

To help remember the five steps, this sentence might be helpful: I MANIFEST THOUGHTS WITH FORGIVENESS AND GRATITUDE. Each of the main words triggers one of the steps.

"*I*" triggers step one to state the qualities you share with nature. "I am abundance."

"*MANIFEST*" triggers step two for stating what you want. "I manifest a $50,000 year net income, or better."

"*THOUGHT*" triggers step three for finding false beliefs and the Truth.

"*FORGIVENESS*" reminds you to locate any grudges and to forgive the people involved.

"*GRATITUDE*" signals the end. You accept what you stated you want with gratitude.

As soon as you have finished the five steps, open up your journal, and write out each mind treatment you did. That means, write out the qualities you share with nature, what you want, the false beliefs and the Truth, the grudges that stand in the way along with forgiveness, and your acceptance with gratitude. Include any other pertinent information you receive during the process.

Writing down *The Mind Treatment* is important. It etches the thought into your brain. It also makes it easy to reinforce your resolution by reviewing them at least once a week.

Of course, mind treatments are just the beginning. You must also barge into action to bring about what you want. In most cases the action will be in steps, and you know how to discover the steps. It is the same as discovering steps to reach any goal.

Use *The Mind Treatment* frequently with confidence and with child-like anticipation of all you can bring into your life.

THE MIND TREATMENT

Begin with ten minutes of The Fundamental Habit. Then with the money rhythm in your awareness, go through the five steps.

STEP ONE: Think of some of your qualities you share with nature. Use the words "I am."

STEP TWO: State clearly in the present tense what you want. Use the words "I manifest" and include "or better" where possible. State only the believable.

STEP THREE: Using "Yes" and "No" signals as an aid, discover any false beliefs that could keep you from manifesting your desire, along with the Truth. Devise an instant ritual to heal and release the false beliefs and to substitute the Truth.

STEP FOUR: Using the "Yes" and "No" signals as an aid, discover the grudges that stand in your way. Forgive the people involved using The Act Of Forgiveness.

STEP FIVE: Accept with gratitude what you are manifesting.

Remember these five steps with this sentence: I MANIFEST THOUGHTS WITH FORGIVENESS AND GRATITUDE.

Chapter Fourteen

Ethics and Principles

You are now in tune with the incredible power of nature. All of its forces are at your command.

It is just a matter of waking up to cosmic energy. It is part of you—nay, it is you. The most fundamental unit in the cosmos, The Unified Field, is your basis. It is that basis which is your power.

All that there is in creation came about by stirring The Unified Field. Onto a field of absolute silence where there appears to be nothing, your thoughts reverberate. They activate that silence into vibration, just as electrical impulses set a speaker into vibration.

The Unified Field is first stirred by the vibration of thought. Once it gets started, the vibration grows larger and more complex, building upon itself. It continues to be shaped by your thought that activated it, but it is also influenced by all your other thoughts, by the thoughts in mass-consciousness, and by cosmic intelligence. In that way the world you experience comes about.

The more focused and the more powerful your thought is, the faster and easier the results. Power comes from belief, determination, and being in the flow.

We manifest by attracting to us those vibrations in tune with our thoughts. If we intend to get an automobile, the means to get it open up. Thought vibrations activate nature to spring desire into reality.

By being in touch with The Unified Field we are in touch with the most powerful center in the universe. Just by being in touch with it, we inherit and harness its power.

The more refined aspects of nature are more powerful. When humankind split the atom, we witnessed a hint of the forces in the internal regions of creation. The Unified Field is the most refined, and we can't begin to imagine its magnitude. Its power is infinite. Everything that can be imagined can be manifested from there.

This power is yours for the asking, but it comes with strings attached. You must be flowing with nature. As long as you stay in tune with nature, the power is your willing servant. Abuse it or misuse it, and you will loose it. This is a basic law. That is why so many people are not wallowing in wealth like the human blueprint provides.

Consider the story of Adam and Eve. They flowed with nature in the Garden of Eden. All the forces of nature were there to serve them their rightful fruits. Somehow they abused the power. Whatever they did, they lost their flow with nature and her support. Then they were left to fend for themselves. They evidently didn't know it, but their loss was temporary. They could have tuned back into the forces of nature at any time.

The same is true with modern man. Until we realign ourselves with the fundamental energies of nature, life is a struggle, and poverty is all too common. That is totally unnecessary. Humanity simply needs to return to the flow.

Returning to the flow is what you are doing with your new techniques. This has a profound significance in your life, and it influences all of humanity. Your awareness of your own power and of the flow of nature touches everyone. To some degree, you bring everyone closer to the flow each time you do *The Fundamental Habit* because the orderliness of The Unified Field has such a great impact on mass-consciousness. Furthermore, the more other people are in the flow, the greater is a single influence. Eventually everyone shifts into the flow automatically without even realizing what happened. That is your supreme gift to humanity by just practicing your new techniques.

We can give back to humanity their Garden of Eden. In that garden—an enlightened world—abundance is the rule, not exception. I have no doubt that we are on the verge of such a life on this planet. And you are one of the key players, even though your main motivation for learning these techniques is to get richer. Indeed you will. At the same time everyone else will get richer also.

As I mentioned, the fruits of the flow come with strings. Your new power can not be misused. Your actions must always be in accordance with the highest good of the earth and all her inhabitants. If you fall short, your power wanes. There is no probation or grace period. Whatever you do must be in accord with the laws of nature.

This isn't a burden. In fact, it takes more effort to lose the power than to keep it. It takes more effort to paddle up-stream than to float down-stream.

By practicing the techniques in this book, you flow with nature, and you stay in the flow. All your goals you discovered are in the flow for the highest common good. Your guidance for each step toward your goal leads you only to supportive activity. Nevertheless, it behooves all of us to double check if there is any doubt.

Verifying The Highest Good is quite easy. During the last ten minutes of *The Fundamental Habit*, ask, "Is so-and-so in the highest and wisest interest for the earth and her inhabitants?" If no, find out why. A simple revision might be all that is needed.

There is another technique to verify your actions are for the highest good. This is your negative-action signal. Most of you already have one, but may not realize it until it is revealed. Then you'll recognize it and remember some of the moments you've felt it. With this signal you know before you do something if it goes against your best interest or if it is harmful to the planet or other people.

When I'm about to do something inappropriate, I get an uncomfortable tingle in the back of my head. Whenever I ignore the signal, the outcome is not what I want.

Discovering Your Negative-Action Signal is the same procedure you used to get your other signals. Begin *The Fundamental Habit*. In the last ten minutes say, "Give me a negative-action signal." You will notice some sensation that is uncomfortable. It probably won't be a movement, since you want to feel this signal in full activity.

If this procedure doesn't give you the desired results, go through the steps set out for *Discovering Your Money Rhythm*, asking instead for a negative-action signal.

I have felt my negative-action signal when I was about to write an unwise letter. I've felt it when I was about to speak my mind in anger. I've felt it when I was about to go into an unwise business deal. The signal can come any time, and it always means to reexamine what you're about to do. It may mean you should abandon your idea, but it could also mean you only need to modify your thinking. The best way to find out is to ask. After ten minutes of *The Fundamental Habit*, ask about your anticipated action. Use your "Yes" and "No" signals as an aid in getting answers.

There is an important principle you need to incorporated into your life to guarantee wealth. This is the principle of letting money flow through you. Don't be a dam for the flowing current. Don't hoard. Instead, develop the attitude you are wading in a stream of money. Its source is out of sight, but unlimited. It just keeps flowing. If you knew a stream never stopped flowing, you wouldn't dam it up just for the water. You would dam it up only when you felt insecure and thought the water would stop flowing. A fear you won't have enough money and a need to hoard stops the flow of wealth.

When you finally realize that money is energy which has its basis in The Unified Field, then you won't need to hoard. When you finally experience abundance flow to you simply because of *The Fundamental Habit*, then you won't even think of hoarding.

So, in managing your money, develop the habit of letting money flow through you. There are three guidelines to follow. First, put your money to work where it can do the most good. Second, spend at least twenty percent of it. Third, give at least ten percent away.

A lot has been written about giving away money. Too often the proponents are after your money, so their suggestion is tainted with suspicion. Nevertheless, giving away money attracts more money. It keeps the flow moving.

I have a client who is a red-neck oil man with no particular philosophy or religion. By experience he knows he must give away fifty percent of everything he earns, or his income severely dips. One year he nearly panicked because he didn't see how he could give enough away. On paper he had made a million dollars, but he was cash shy. So he borrowed five hundred thousand dollars. This man swears his wealth is predicated on giving away the fifty percent, and he doesn't take any chances.

Giving is fun. You don't have to pick charities, unless you're after a tax deduction. You can give fifty dollar bills to the street people who approach you. You can give your paper boy a hefty tip. You can fix up a poor person's apartment. This is heart warming. Of course, giving to the arts, hospitals, schools, missions, and the host of charities is also rewarding. The point is to give. Just because it is fun or a cause you believe in does not diminish its effect.

These two principles are basic to everyone. Everything you do must benefit humankind, the earth, and her inhabitants. You must also let money flow though you, not just to you. Always keep these two principles at the surface of your awareness.

These are the only two principles I'm going to emphasize. This is not a treatise on precisely what to think or what to do. This book is only meant to empower. From there you write your own script. The knowledge you need is within you. The principles or ethics you need to work on or emphasize become evident. Any list I might come up with would be incomplete for you. Worse yet, such a list might appear exhaustive, and you wouldn't come up with your own.

Your next exercise is to do just that: *Discovering Your Ethics And Principles*. After ten minutes of *The Fundamental Habit*, ask for the ethics and principles you need to keep in mind. They might be principles you're ignoring and need to relearn. They might be principles that come up often. Or, they just might be universal principles we all need to keep in mind as our contribution to mass-consciousness. Of course, verify that they are correct with the aid of your "Yes" and "No" signals. Use as many sessions as you need to get a complete list.

Write down each ethic or principle in your journal as soon as you receive it. If you wait until afterward, you run the risk of forgetting it. If you know, also write why each is important for you to keep in mind.

Think of your ethics and principles frequently. Review your list occasionally. Above all, incorporate them into your business and personal life.

These principles are the backbone of your wealth. Let the wisdom of your ethics be etched into your consciousness.

VERIFYING YOUR HIGHEST GOOD

STEP ONE: Ten minutes of The Fundamental Habit.

STEP TWO: Ask, "Is (state activity) in the highest and wisest interest for the earth and all her inhabitants?" Use your "Yes" and "No" signals as an aid.

STEP THREE: If the answer is no, find out why. A simple revision may be all that is necessary.

The total time for each session should be twenty minutes.

DISCOVERING YOUR NEGATIVE-ACTION SIGNAL

STEP ONE: Ten minutes of The Fundamental Habit.

STEP TWO: Ask for a negative-action signal. You will notice an uncomfortable sensation that can be repeated easily in activity. Write a description of it in your journal.

Note: If you want, go through the steps for Discovering Your Money Rhythm, asking instead for a negative-action signal.

DISCOVERING YOUR ETHICS AND PRINCIPLES

STEP ONE: Ten minutes of The Fundamental Habit.

STEP TWO: Ask for the ethics and principles that are appropriate for you to keep in mind. Use your "Yes" and "No" signals to verify what you receive in your thoughts.

STEP THREE: Write the ethics and principles in your journal. Review them periodically, and keep them in mind.

The total time for each session should be twenty minutes.

Chapter Fifteen

The Practice Revisited

This book presents a very different approach for making money. One one hand it is new and revolutionary. On another hand it is as old as creation itself. The simple techniques put you in touch with the extravagance of nature. Once in touch, you manifest with focused, powerful, and wise thoughts a life of abundance.

This knowledge seems new because modern society does not flow with nature. The knowledge is old because humans are created with the ability to share in the easy flow of wealth the universe provides.

For most of recorded history human life is characterized as a struggle. "Nature" represents forces to be conquered and overcome. Except in a few "primitive" cultures, there is little effort to emulate nature or to let natural law work for us. We opt to ignore the greatest energies and our most powerful friend.

Nature is so much more than we perceive. More than the forests. More than the oceans. More than the skies. More, much more, than the multifarious forms around us. Nature extends to the far reaches of the universe. Nature also extends inward to the smallest, most elementary particles and fields.

Most of nature, from the outer reaches to the most elementary particles, we have ignored. If not ignored, then we tried to change. We took, we demanded, we pilfered, we polluted, but we haven't flowed.

The results of such an attitude have put us in a dangerous situation. People are starving. Whole species of plants and animals are going extinct at alarming rates. Rain forests are being leveled. Water has become undrinkable. Air is suffocating. The protective shield of the earth's atmosphere is deteriorating. Natural resources are being depleted. We could go on to fill up ten pages just enumerating the price of our ignorance.

We people are a strange lot. In spite of all these problems, we somehow still believe we are the most civilized, most advanced people to walk the earth. If we get any more civilized, we're likely to blow the planet into smithereens

What humankind is doing is not civilized. Just concerning wealth, we are in the dark ages. Goods, services, and natural resources are not being distributed to most of earth's people. Only a small percentage live outside poverty. Why? Where did we go wrong?

The answer is simple. We as a people forgot our connection to The Unified Field. We forgot our inherent power. We forgot to flow with almighty creation. We forgot how to live.

Now you have a practice to learn to remember. You can remember to flow with nature. You can remember your connection to The Unified Field. You can remember how to live.

I say "remember" because you are not learning anything new. You are simply revitalizing the forces that are in and around you and that never went away. When these forces are renewed in your life, it is packed with abundance. Your life becomes purposeful and fulfilling.

When greater numbers of people practice these techniques, the whole world will change. Wealth will be distributed fairly. Our actions will stop polluting and destroying nature. Age-old ethics and principles will regain acceptance. This is the automatic effect of an enlightened society, a society flowing with the cosmos.

I don't mean to imply the practice I'm outlining in this book is "the" path. It is a valuable path that works, and it is so easy anyone with or without religious connections can do it.

There are many paths that can bring a person into harmony with the vibrations of nature. This technique qualifies as one because it does just that. By doing that, it opens you up to wealth which is more far reaching than you imagine. Before exploring in the next section how far reaching wealth can be, let's review the practice.

First and foremost you have *The Fundamental Habit.* For twenty minutes before breakfast and again before dinner, sit comfortably with your eyes closed. Your money rhythm will appear. Allow your attention to be with it the entire time. If your mind wanders away on thoughts, then easily come back to the awareness of the money rhythm. Thoughts can be there also; just slightly favor the money rhythm. During the second ten minutes you can ask questions or narrate Truth like you've learned. When the session is over, take another couple of minutes to come out slowly. Not to do so may cause some irritability.

The Fundamental Habit is the most important thing you can do each day. Regularity is key to its effectiveness. Even if you do nothing else, all areas of your life will improve, including the main goal of this Course to get richer.

In order to truly reap the rewards of abundance, you must also come to grips with anger. It can cut you off from nature. Anger is foreign to nature. When you're angry, there is no way you can also flow into money. Yes, I know there are lots of angry people who have lots of money, but their money can leave as fast as it came. Several names may come to your mind to illustrate that point.

Remember those four sentences you think whenever you're angry? They dissolve and neutralize tension. Just think of the people involved and say, "I give you my love; I give you my heart; I receive your love; I receive your heart." These are truly precious words. They smooth out a past problem or something happening in the moment. These words need to be at your fingertips and used without hesitation as often as the urge arises.

Grudges are a form of anger. They can also separate you from the flow—from being in tune with life, nature, and our rightful heritage. We feel a grudge when we think we have been made a lesser person, we've been injured, or something we own has been damaged.

What we fail to realize is that we played a role in whatever happened, and that there is a silver lining to everything that happens to us. If we look closely enough, we'll see some benefit from the experience we hold the grudge over. Look for that silver lining. If it isn't obvious, find out what it is during *The Fundamental Habit*.

To dissolve a grudge, think of the person or people involved, along with the silver lining. Forgive by saying to them those four precious sentences. Forgiveness is just giving love, nothing else. There is no need to forget, and there is no need to confront anyone. It all happens within your own thoughts when you think the four sentences.

Now that you are in the flow with all your anger and grudges under control, you can set about directing the flow. Simply doing *The Fundamental Habit* without anger and without grudges is mighty powerful. A flow of wealth is inevitable from that alone. Events, and people, and coincidences, and opportunities happen. At first you'll be amazed, but soon you'll get used to it. Life can be fun. Indeed it is meant to be fun, and it is more fun when you create.

The first step in creating is to set goals. These are broad overall objectives for your life, for five years, for the next year, for one day, or for any future time. You discover your highest and wisest goals by accessing cosmic intelligence during *The Fundamental Habit*.

In similar fashion you discover a plan of action for each goal. Within you someplace, perhaps in a deep recess of the brain, is an "inner-computer" that always has a clear plan for every goal. With every change that affects your goal, your "inner-computer" spontaneously adjusts the plan of action. To get it, all you need to do is access that computer. During the second ten minutes of *The Fundamental Habit*, ask for the next step to accomplish your goal. The answer will come in your thoughts with perhaps several options Choose one, and then do the action. That is all there is to your plan of action: ask for a step, make a choice from the options, then do the action before asking for the next step.

Both your intellect and your intuition get involved in the fun of creating with *The Mind Treatment*. It brings power and punch to your goals and plans. Take a goal or a step in your plan of action, and focus your thoughts toward its accomplishment with this special technique.

The Mind Treatment requires you to use what you've learned in this Course. Find out if what you want is in your highest and wisest interest, if you have any false beliefs standing in your way, and if any grudges need to be forgiven. Then go through the five steps.

In spite of your new techniques to flow comfortably and easily to wealth, you must make a conscious effort to retain high ethics and principles. This means you must always be on guard that everything you do is in the highest and wisest interest for yourself, for the earth and for her inhabitants. If there is any doubt in your mind, find out during the second ten minutes of *The Fundamental Habit*.

There are always some ethics and principles you need to be reminded of. Some are those you're ignoring. Others are simply important. You made a list, so keep it current. Check periodically during *The Fundamental Habit* to see if new ones should be added. If you ignore ethics and principles, you jeopardize the flow and your rightful abundance.

As a precaution, develop a negative-action signal. You can get this for the asking, like you got your money rhythm. It is an unpleasant sensation that you feel when you're about to do something unwise or inappropriate. Cultivate that signal and follow its guidance.

This is your practice. Let each of its parts become an integral part of your life. Treat the techniques with a degree of reverence, as if your life depends on it. A wealthy, life just might.

Part III

The Ramifications

Chapter Sixteen

The Wealth of Possessions

We equate the word "wealth" with possessions. A wealthy person is one who owns lots of things. The wealthy control assets, have much money, and purchase what they want with little consideration of cost.

When we say people are not wealthy, we usually mean they have few possessions, little money, a mediocre income, and mountains of debt. They purchase with bargain coupons, shop sales, and buy the generic.

This is the commonly held view of wealth. Certainly, money and possessions are an aspect of wealth, but it is far, far more. Such a limited view actually will inhibit the flow of wealth.

People often feel poor, when in fact they are wallowing in wealth. Those feelings create their reality. They bring sad feelings of failure, of lack, of low self esteem, of unfulfilled desires, and of being poor providers.

To be in the flow brings an expanded awareness of the many forms of abundance in our life.

In this Part III we explore that expanded vision. We examine the abundance of nature, of the earth, of your own Self, and of your creation. We find perfection, extravagance, unlimited resources, infinite potential, and fun.

By doing *The Fundamental Habit* twice daily, you have put yourself in touch with The Unified Field. This is the basis of everything, and whatever you own is just an expression of The Unified Field. Everything in creation shares the same elementary building block.

As a young boy, I was taught the most elementary unit in creation is the atom. Now I know everything boils down to some form of vibration. More basic still is the simplest vibration, the sine wave.

Even the sine wave, while basic to all of our material world is not the state of least excitation. That state, or field, is actually perfect silence. No motion and no activity exists whatsoever there. Yet within it resides the potential for everything imaginable. Everything arises from it. And "it" is what Einstein called The Unified Field.

The Unified Field is the basis of time, space, gravitation, matter, and energy. This concept makes the universe so simple that our complex intellects can not comprehend it fully. It is like trying to grasp a cloud or a hologram. To grasp it is to grasp the nature of our Selves. That is like the eye looking at itself.

To understand your own nature is to understand creation. To dabble with creation is to play with the mechanics of creating. That is the gift you've given yourself with your twice daily routine of *The Fundamental Habit*. You have put yourself in the direct flow of creating. You are in tune with the basic creating energies so you can stir The Unified Field. And you stir it with your thoughts.

You can't stir the stew until you put the spoon in the pot. *The Fundamental Habit* is putting the spoon in the pot. Your intention to create something is analogous to stirring the stew—your intention stirs The Unified Field. This is how you begin to create whatever you want.

You are developing the ability to create anything from the flow of nature. Just as nature proliferates abundance, so too do you. The only requirement is that you are in the flow. When you are in the flow, you only desire to create what is most supportive for yourself and for everyone else, and the highest ethics and principles protect you from receiving or inflicting harm. The result is extravagant abundance. After all, nature herself is extravagantly abundant. She does not deny you anything she has when you are flowing with her.

To manifest material wealth, first come up with a wise goal during *The Fundamental Habit.* Then uncover initial options for the first action you need to do, make a choice, and do it. Then uncover the next option, make a choice, and act. And so it goes. It is that simple. You need only be certain that your goals are correct for you and that each step unfolds one at a time like you were taught. You can't fail. In this way you create your own world of material abundance.

This basic practice naturally leads to expanded awareness of your rich, varied, and abundant environment. One of the first symptoms of this expanded awareness is an overwhelming appreciation of beauty.

For instance, take flowers. You are bound to experience an expanded awareness of them. As simple as this sounds, that is expanding your wealth. Each flower is a material possession. They're all around you. They are jewels of the plant kingdom for your natural adornment. Pick them. Smell them. Feel them. Admire them. Talk to them. Allow the billions of flowers to be part of your abundance because they are.

It the same with trees. Your expanded awareness opens you up to feel their spirit and your commonality with them. After all, you and the trees are expressions of the same Unified Field, yet you now appreciate the uniqueness and seemingly infinite expressions of these giant plants. To be in the flow is to notice, love, and accept all the plant kingdom into your material world. How wealthy each person on earth would be to do just that.

You are also broadening your awareness for animals. Without even thinking about it, you are appreciating all of nature more and more every day. Continue to let your awareness grow. Notice insects you didn't know existed. Marvel at the sounds of birds, a true orchestra. Speak to dogs, cats, even rabbits and gophers, with a sense of rapport. No animal belongs exclusively to someone. All are expressions of nature, and they are all part of your material wealth. Incorporate them into your world, and enjoy the contribution each makes. Bees and flies are incredibly beautiful. Focus on that beauty. It brings a feeling of awe money can't buy.

You are also incorporating an appreciation of public wealth into your life. All cities are laden with parks. There are libraries. Your government runs museums and recreation facilities, like swimming pools, ball parks, jogging trails, senior citizen clubhouses, and beaches. These are part of your abundance. When you are in the flow, these resources are automatically inventoried as part of your material world.

The appreciation of wealth from public property underscores another point. You can't truly appreciate your abundance unless everyone else around you is abundant. Since we all share in the abundance of flowers, trees, animals, and public facilities, we can begin to feel abundant with everyone else. Gone is the notion that you are wealthy when you own more than most other people. That is tantamount to hoarding which stops the flow.

To accept wealth for everyone does not mean in the least that we are to live a communal world. No. We can keep the concepts of private property. You have abundance because of your flow with nature. Other people also have wealth when they're in the flow. There are enough resources on earth now for everyone to live abundant lives. The only requirement for each person is to be in the flow.

A significant ramification of *The Fundamental Habit* is that you are helping to bring the world out of poverty. The reason lies in the nature of our connection to everyone else. You can't stir The Unified Field without stirring it for everyone else. To some degree you improve everyone's power to manifest as you improve your own. The more people stirring The Unified Field with this or some other technique, the greater will be the effect. In that way, a small number of people lift everyone up to abundance.

That idea can be mind boggling. Inherent in getting into the flow is a world wide solution to famine and scarcity. Nature is abundance. When some of us flow with nature, everyone inherits the results.

Another ramification of your practice is a form of wealth called "skill-in-action." What is it worth to waste no time in reaching a goal? A friend of mine had just started these techniques when she had to move to another apartment. She came up with a goal: an apartment with a view, top floor, large, one bedroom, security parking, and a certain price. Then she discovered the first step: bicycle through a particular neighborhood to jot down likely buildings. Within two hours she had her apartment.

That is "skill-in-action." She wasted no time. She rode directly to the apartment, as if led.

What is such skill worth? It is impossible to put a dollar value on it, but it is clearly part of our wealth. I started watching my friend more closely after that. Indeed, she accomplished everything with the same ease.

It boils down to accomplishing more by doing less. That leaves more time and resources for other projects. Material wealth is your birthright. It comes naturally and easily with the regular practice of *The Fundamental Habit*. You expand your awareness of the wealth around you, and you manifest your true goals with efficient and fine tuned skill.

Wealth comes to you quite spontaneously. You don't need to try, or work harder, or go through a myriad of changes. You simply need to get into the rhythmic flow of nature's vibration. That is the gift of these techniques.

Furthermore, you gain wealth without hoarding or depriving others. Indeed it is the opposite. As you gain more possessions by being in the flow, you open up the flow for everyone to some degree. That is the nature of life. For centuries we've been pulling each other away from the flow and into deprivation. Now we can push each other into the flow and into abundance.

Chapter Seventeen

The Wealth of Health

We don't usually link health with wealth, but we should. The amount of money we spend on our bodies is enormous. From lotions to pills, from reducing salons to special diets, from doctors to acupuncturists, from medical insurance to hospitals, from gyms to jogging shoes, from vitamins to organic foods, we constantly spend on health.

J. Paul Getty said if he had known he would live so long, he would have taken better care of himself. Health is wealth. Many people would gladly trade all their material wealth for health wealth. Health can be enjoyed without possessions, but possessions can't be enjoyed without health.

Health is so valuable we often try to buy it. My father bought a new hip. His roommate in the hospital bought two new knees. With fore-sight we try to buy wellness in advance. Thirty dollars a month for aerobics is health maintenance. Fifty dollars for a dental cleaning is health maintenance. Ten dollars for sun block is health maintenance. Health is a possession we're willing to pay for. Increasingly we invest for future health.

Health is the foundation for all our other possessions. That is, enjoy-ment of anything is predicated on being healthy. Obviously, if we're sick in bed, a whole collection of exotic cars would just sit in the garage.

Good health is the basis of how we perceive our world. Take a sunset. If you have a headache, its beauty is lost. You may not even notice it. Whatever is going on around you must be perceived. Otherwise it is not part of your life. What you perceive and how you interact with it is governed by your health, both physical and mental.

I purposely stood on a crowded street the other day to watch what went on around me. A dog chased another, until they both took off after a cat. A homeless woman moved her grocery cart across the street. Two girls in purple hair and black leather pumps meandered by. An ice cream vendor rang a bell and shouted his flavors. An aggressive pigeon landed on a man's hand filled with crumbs. A taxi, horn blaring, barely missed a bicyclist. Yet, no-one noticed any of it.

People are absorbed in their own fears and fantasies. Their minds race a mile a minute about events that could happen but probably won't, about misunderstanding what someone said, or about their aches and pains.

Most of your friends miss the world around them because their body hurts or their mind is confused. That absorbs most of their attention. Thoughts about something that makes them afraid crowds out their sunsets. Simple misunderstandings paint out their beautiful world.

Your state of mind and your state of body are important aspects of your wealth, maybe the most important. Without both mental and physical health, you can not enjoy your possessions. If they aren't the source of fun, happiness, and creativity, why have them?

Poor health has a devastating effect on our thoughts. We've all experienced that. We can fly off the handle with the slightest provocation when we're under the weather.

What you think, you will own. What you think will become your reality. Rotten apples in, rotten apples out. Garbage in, garbage out.

Poor health can be the foundation for angry, unproductive, revengeful, doubting, cynical, and confused thoughts. Those thoughts manifest. They bring experiences clothed in anger, revenge, doubts, cynicism, and confusion.

Even when sick, you are responsible for your thoughts and therefore what they manifest in your life. That is the reality that drives home the value of your health.

Is it a mere coincidence of semantics that five sixths of the word *health* is contained in the word *wealth*? Or that five sixths of *wealth* is in *health*?

To be successful, any system to bring wealth into your life must also be a system to bring health. It would be useless to own a car on an island with no service stations and no mechanics. You wouldn't enjoy the car without the necessary support facilities. Health is support for wealth. Without health, wealth is useless. It would bring you no joy and no fun. It can't even bring you a sense of accomplishment or a desire to share. Wealth without health is like skis without snow.

These techniques you've learned for bringing abundance into your life provide a wealth support system. You have all you need in order to get, maintain, expand, and enjoy your possessions. Clearly, that would have to include good health.

And, indeed it does. Haven't you noticed better health since regularly practicing *The Fundamental Habit*? Perfect health is a natural outgrowth of being in tune with nature.

Just look at nature. She is constantly trying to fix whatever is out of balance. No matter what we do, nature doubles her efforts to mend, heal, and correct. That is natural law. Equilibrium and balance are to be maintained. Everything is constantly seeking its normal condition. This never stops.

Forests grow back after a fire. New species are mutated to replace extinct ones. Our bodies develop new antibodies to combat strange viruses. Nature constantly corrects, balances, protects, and heals.

When you zero in on the money rhythm, you focus on nature with all of her regenerative powers. More than material wealth is attracted into your life. You are also attracting healing energies that restore balance.

Nature always provides whatever is needed to meet its objective. That is the nature of nature; that is the nature of The Unified Field; that is the nature of the money rhythm. It comes equipped to bring you the health you need to assure material abundance.

Any physical or mental abnormalities will be corrected. You don't have to know how to correct the problem. You don't even have to know the problem exists. Quite automatically physical and mental abnormalities are healed. Then you can wallow in the abundance you're supposed to have.

These automatic corrections in your health are made with no fanfare. They come without your realizing it. You might notice fewer colds, headaches, or sinus attacks. You might notice the onset of the flu, only to see it pass quickly. Expect this, and make a special point to watch for health improvements. Make note of them in your journal. They are easy to miss, so you need to give it thoughtful attention.

Another way you improve your health is by changing your habits. No, you won't have to make a list of them. We don't dwell on bad habits—or even identify them, for that matter. Bad habits gradually and automatically lose their appeal with *The Fundamental Habit*.

Even your mental outlook improves. You find yourself immersed in the beauty around you. Street scenes can become a place of intrigue and adventure, while they used to be only a place to get from here to there.

Differing viewpoints can be appreciated without misunderstandings. Imagined fears are replaced by realistic observations. Whatever clouds your thinking and pollutes your thoughts is cleansed away. The result is a brighter, more optimistic outlook in a varied and exciting life.

All these benefits to better health come about naturally without trying to do anything. You need only *The Fundamental Habit* twice a day.

I do not mean to suggest you will never need medical care. You may. Whenever you get sick, do everything that is reasonable and available to get well. That includes seeing a doctor. Don't leave any stone unturned.

When you're working through a medical problem, you can transpose your money rhythm into your "Perfect Health Rhythm" with your mere intention. Just think of the money rhythm as being your perfect health rhythm. With the renaming and your intention to heal something specific, you accelerate nature's own healing process.

Some people prefer to have a separate perfect health rhythm, and it is easy to get. During *The Fundamental Habit*, ask for it. Another distinct rhythm will appear.

Think of your health as wealth. When your body and your mind are in perfect operating condition, you are at your optimum for creating your material world and for enjoying it. Perfect health need not be a luxury. It is a normal human condition. It is the foundation for a fulfilling, wealthy life.

Chapter Eighteen

The Wealth of Relationships

The experience of wealth begins with *The Fundamental Habit* and focusing on the money rhythm to flow with nature. During the practice you discover a wise goal concerning money and the first step to take to accomplish the goal. After completing the action required for the step, you discover the next step. And so it goes until the goal is fulfilled.

The mechanics to bring a fulfilling relationship into your life are the same: *The Fundamental Habit*, discovering a wise goal, discovering the first step, action, discovering the next step, action, and so on.

The same principles operate because relationships are a form of wealth. They are assets. Your life would be empty without relationships. They give it flavor. Each person in your life is like a special spice.

When we think of relationships, we usually think of spouses, lovers, dates, and affairs. While they are important, they are only a segment. Comfortable and supportive people need to be around you in all your activities. Without such support your projects won't bear much fruit. Life wouldn't be much fun, either.

There is no way you can do these techniques without attracting perfect people. Most of the steps to accomplish your goals require certain people to appear.

If your goal is a perfect job with a good income, obviously all kinds of people will come into your life. There may be personnel managers, supervisors, co-workers, clients, or customers. Some people come just to show you the way. Each of these people enter into a unique relationship with you, and each is just the right person. The people you need to fulfill the goal will flow to you as easily as water flows down a hillside. The process is automatic. This is a necessary ramification of your new techniques. It comes as part of the wealth support system. There is nothing else for you to do. People come spontaneously as part of the flow. We all move into each others lives to provide ideas, resources, support, help, and love.

At some time or other you may want someone special. It might be a Mister or Miss Right. It could also be a best friend. Or it might be a companion or nurse. You might want a gardener, housekeeper, or even a butler.

When it is a wise goal to find someone special, use the money rhythm during *The Fundamental Habit* with the intention of finding that perfect lover, perfect housekeeper, perfect companion, perfect best friend, etc. By your intention, the money rhythm becomes a perfect relationship rhythm. If you prefer, you can go after a specific relationship rhythm, just like you could get a specific perfect health rhythm.

You may want to devote a portion of each session of *The Fundamental Habit* to relationships. After a few minutes, change to the relationship rhythm, either with your intention or the separate rhythm. This helps to manifest someone particular or to insure smoothness in all your relationships.

The Fundamental Habit with a relationship rhythm helps you to flow to and with the perfect people. At the same time, don't forget to discover wise relationship goals and each step to fulfill them. *The Mind Treatment* also adds punch to the process.

When it comes to manifesting perfect relationships, be diligent in allowing the flow to carry you. Intend to manifest the perfect lover, or whomever, but don't be more specific. Too often we decide we want a certain person in our life. That attitude interferes with the other person's free will. Furthermore, it tries to override the process of naturally flowing with nature and with what is in our highest and wisest interest. If we flow, the people that come to us are the very best, taking into consideration all the countless factors.

Relationships are wealth. A rich person without satisfying relationships has a lonely life. That is not acceptable, and there is no excuse for it.

The process is simple. Bring The Unified Field into your life. Flow with nature. You surely will attract perfect people in every arena of your life.

Chapter Nineteen

The Wealth of Love

We equate our feeling of love with a lover or someone close. When the lover isn't there, we commonly experience a void of love in our lives. That void is a misconception.

"I am in love with you." "You have brought love into my life." "Our love is forever." "I want all your love."

These expressions presuppose an object for our love. But love just is. The feeling just exists. What we call love is from ourselves. It doesn't come from the other person. Love needs no object. We can feel love even in solitary confinement.

Wouldn't it be nice to have the feeling of love all the time, with or without a lover? We can. It is a natural feeling from a nervous system that is operating at peak performance. Love is the feeling we get when we are aware of The Unified Field. When we experience our most basic nature, we feel love. The Unified field is love.

Being aware of your Self is being aware of The Unified Field. You are The Unified Field, and when your awareness includes that field, you are in tune with all of nature, indeed all of creation. This means harmony and easy flowing. A natural feeling of love pops up in that harmony.

When you first tried *The Basic Practice*, you probably noticed a feeling of love. It may even have lingered for several hours. If you haven't experienced this love feeling yet, the regular and continued practice of

The Fundamental Habit will bring it about. That is as certain as the coming of the full moon.

The feeling of love builds upon itself. That is, the longer you do *The Fundamental Habit*, the more you'll experience the love feeling. It is in direct proportion to the degree to which you experience The Unified Field. That is precisely what you are feeling—The Unified Field.

When you put your hand in warm water and stir it, you feel warmth. When you don't move your hand, eventually you feel nothing. Like the water around your hand, The Unified Field surrounds you at all times. It is above, below, right, left, front, back, and within. There is no place it is not, but it is only felt when it is stirred.

Becoming very relaxed with *The Fundamental Habit* stirs The Unified Field. Your creative centers are enlivened. The Unified Field begins its dance in the neurons of your nervous system. What you feel is called love.

The Unified Field is love. Love is the most elementary ingredient in the universe. Everything is love. To feel The Unified field—love—is to feel creation. It is indeed amazing that we are able to feel such a profound level of creation.

What a ramification this is! We begin with a simple technique to flow with abundance, and we end up feeling love!

Nevertheless, this is a natural benefit of *The Fundamental Habit*. As you get more into the flow with nature and as your health improves, your nervous system becomes more refined. It is able to pick up more subtle vibrations. With a little practice, your nervous system picks up the most subtle vibration of all, the feeling of The Unified Field, the feeling of love.

Eventually the feeling never goes away. It becomes a permanent condition. Whatever is happening around you, the feeling remains. "But I want to experience sadness, or frustration, or sorrow, and all the other human emotions. I don't want to only feel love," you might think. Of course! To experience human wholeness means to experience all of the human emotions. Just because you can always experience love does not keep you from having the full range of emotions.

Love is not one of the human emotions. It appears to be because it comes and goes for most of us like emotions do. We think love gives way to loneliness, or visa versa. In truth, love can always be there. Love is omnipresent for all time because The Unified Field is omnipresent for all time. Losing contact with The Unified Field is the only reason we could lose the feeling of love.

Love is an overlay. It can be in your awareness as a backdrop for every other emotion and for whatever you are doing. Stop the flow, and the feeling stops. Flow, and the feeling is there. It is that simple.

Clearly, love requires no object. You don't have to love someone or something to feel it. Love just is. It always just is. How is it then that you do fall in love with someone? It appears the person somehow created your feeling of love.

Remember, I have stated several times that there are infinite paths to enliven our awareness of The Unified Field. One such path is certainly *The Fundamental Habit*. Another path is falling in love with someone. We can contact The Unified Field using the path of our intimate relationships. It has that power. No wonder then that we place so much value on "falling in love." Those words are no coincidence. You fall into The Unified Field—fall into love.

Like all techniques to cultivate The Unified Field, you need to do it regularly and continuously. On that score the "falling in love" technique often misses the mark. We get into ruts and lose the intrigue and romance. We're disillusioned because the feeling disappears. That need not be the case, but you would have to work at the romance to keep it alive. Many people do. They elevate their consciousness and incorporate The Unified Field to flow into their lives with the path of intimate relationships.

An easier and more mechanical path to love is *The Fundamental Habit* twice each day. It brings to you a feeling of love that doesn't go away. The feeling becomes the basis for all your relationships.

When your awareness is anchored in The Unified Field, the feeling of love isn't dependent on someone. Your relationships become freer and more stable. You don't demand your lover, spouse, or friend to supply you with love. It already is there. Such freedom allows your relationships to bloom beyond imagination.

This ramification of *The Fundamental Habit* should be enough incentive to be regular in the practice. People spend fortunes and a lifetime looking for love. Now it can be yours with a little time and perseverance. Nothing else is required.

Chapter Twenty

The Wealth of Peace

Could you believe that peace of mind is a ramification of these techniques? Yes, because you have experienced it. Could you also believe that world peace is a ramification of these techniques? It is. Inherent in your quest for money with these techniques are both aspects of peace: peace of mind and world peace.

We manifest with our thoughts. A turbulent mind with scattered, misdirected thoughts brings us a personal world of chaos. If everyone experiences a turbulent mind, the inevitable result is a turbulent world. There is a definite connection between peace of mind and world peace. They are two sides of the same coin.

Both peace of mind and world peace affect material abundance. A peaceful world cooperates to produce infinite varieties of food and consumer products. An embattled world requires sacrifice while the focus is to produce bombs, guns, and tanks. On the personal side, your experience clearly shows a rise in your own productivity when you are at peace. Under stress, you can't seem to pull it together.

The Unified Field is pure peace. At that level of creation, there is no activity, only potential. Nothing could be quieter, yet nothing is potentially more. In that silence, your thoughts stir "unmanifest" energy to give birth to a world of many and varied expressions.

When you do *The Fundamental Habit*, your conscious mind dips into that "unmanifest" silence. Like dipping a cloth into a die solution, your mind is saturated with The Unified Field in its most pure state, silence. That is ultimate peace, and you bring it back into your life when the session is over. You experience saturation of The Unified Field as peace of mind.

You don't become a zombie. The peace doesn't leave you lethargic. You aren't sleepy and lazy. This peace overlays dynamic activity. You feel confident and energetic.

The infusion of The Unified Field spurs intense activity accompanied with peacefulness. Such a great combination! The result is successful action. Your goals are quickly realized. Your wealth multiplies. Your influence is felt. Life becomes fun because you aren't afraid. Besides, life is always fun when we're being productive without turmoil.

Being productive without turmoil: that is the gift of a peaceful mind.

There is nothing else to learn for this peace. It is there automatically. There is nothing to memorize. There are no new techniques to master. Just do *The Fundamental Habit*. Get into the flow. Dip into The Unified Field. Become one with nature. That's all there is to it.

The "snakes" on the floor of a dark room are seen as mere ropes when a light is turned on. *The Fundamental Habit* is turning on the light. With light you see reality. That is enlightenment. It is nothing more than being infused with the clarity that comes by dipping regularly into The Unified Field.

Regardless of whatever situation you're in, there is a solution. Always. Without exception. There is no problem that can arise in this world that is without solution. The real challenge is to correctly understand the problem. If you think the floor is full of snakes, you can't find a correct solution when the floor is only full of ropes. On the other hand, if they really are snakes, you can get the solution in the normal manner: set a goal and discover the steps one at a time to reach the goal. Every goal can be reached if there is clarity.

Remember that your money rhythm carries with it all the support needed to bring your material wealth. Health is an example; the money rhythm has a built-in health support system. It also has a built-in relationship support system.

The same holds for peace of mind. There is a support system for it within the money rhythm. This is because peace is a prerequisite for flowing with wealth. Without peace, the flow stops, and the role of the money rhythm would be thwarted. Everything the money rhythm needs to bring wealth into your life is inherent in the rhythm and in your techniques for using it.

World peace is a reflection of collective peace of minds. If everyone on earth had peace of mind, war would be absurd. Whenever you take care of your own mind, you raise the possibilities of world peace to some degree. Clearly, the greatest single contribution you can make for world order is to locate and keep the peace of mind that is your birthright.

Furthermore, the principles governing mass-consciousness are also at work. Your state of mind influences everyone else. This is true because we are all connected; we share The Unified Field as a common denominator, and you make an impression in it. It is natural law, however, that you have a greater impact on mass-consciousness when you are at peace than when you're in turmoil. That is just the nature of orderliness. It is many times more powerful than disorderliness.

An example of the power of orderliness is the laser light. It is perfectly ordered light waves, and its beam can go to the moon and back with little loss. On the other hand, the scattered light of an ordinary bulb can be seen for only a few miles.

It is the same with your thoughts. Thoughts emanating from a peaceful, ordered mind inject that peace and order into mass-consciousness. Peace and order negate weak and scattered thoughts many times over. That is the key to world peace. It begins by simply bringing The Unified Field into your own life. It has tremendous effect because a little bit of order injected into mass-consciousness neutralizes tons of its disorder.

If we are ever going to obtain world peace, it will be by applying this natural law. This is understood by important groups around the globe. Many in their own ways are infusing order into mass-consciousness. This has been going on for decades. The effect is being felt, but, obviously, a lot more infusion needs to take place. Your contribution can be significant.

You don't have to think world peace for this to happen. You don't even have to believe it. Just go after your own peace of mind by going after wealth with *The Fundamental Habit*. All the better that world peace naturally follows.

Chapter Twenty-One

The Wealth of the Subconscious

Already you have delved into your subconscious with these techniques. You uncovered rhythms and signals. You discovered false beliefs about money held by you or by society, and you set about to correct them. You examined your subconscious fear-associations.

Even your plan-of-action involved the subconscious. You solicited its input to set your goals and to discover the steps to reach them. You needed your subconscious in coming to grips with anger, grudges, forgiveness, and ethics.

Each step in this Course has enlivened your connection to the subconscious. It is becoming a clear and reliable friend, as it is intended to be.

The subconscious is a warehouse of information. It is connected to the intelligence of nature. It remembers everything about your life. It sets your behavioral patterns. Not a moment goes by that you don't use this silent reservoir of wisdom.

As you discovered, some of the beliefs you put into the subconscious are not correct. While it does know Truth, it also is your devout servant. At your direction, it covers up Truth with your own prejudices, notions, and illusions. You placed many false beliefs into the subconscious on "automatic pilot." That is, you decreed those false beliefs would override Truth and would be your silent manifesting thought.

We all manifest with thoughts that are so deep in our subconscious we don't know they exist. They are in the subconscious because we put them there, if only by acquiescing to the screams of societal beliefs in mass-consciousness.

You may have assumed the subconscious mind is nearly impossible to pierce. Now you have experienced that it is easily accessible. You can learn what is in it, and you can change its program. You can because the subconscious is your faithful servant. You just need a key, and you now have one. There are many keys, but these techniques fit the lock.

You have practiced dipping into the subconscious with the desire to make money. That is just one facet of life, albeit important. All other aspects of your life can also be enriched with these techniques. Use some creativity. Adapt and expand each of the principles. Tap into universal intelligence for guidance in any activity. Open yourself up to a conscious connection to your subconscious in all the realms of human existence. It has knowledge to accomplish anything. Use it.

As openers, try dream analysis. Your subconscious feeds your conscious mind knowledge all the time. One way is with dreams. Each dream is a message, but its message is hidden in symbols. You now have all the tools to find out their meanings.

Keep a paper and pencil at your bedside. As soon as you wake up, write down everything you remember about your dreams. You will probably forget even the clearest dream in a minute, so don't procrastinate. Include colors, shapes, kinds of clothes, types of vehicles, settings, names of plants and animals, and any other distinguishing features.

Each item is a symbol that is unique for you and for each dream. You can't go to a book on dream symbols to interpret your dream. Each symbol is your own subconscious symbol, and it may be very different from someone else's.

After you have the list, use the techniques you've learned to tap the knowledge of your subconscious. That is, start with *The Fundamental Habit* for ten minutes. Then ask questions, verifying with your "Yes" and "No" signals. Find out what the symbols mean. Let the meaning of the dreams unfold. You will be amazed at how much you learn about your direction in life, your focus, and your strengths. It is truly a liberating experience.

Keep a list of your symbols and their meanings in your journal. Don't be surprised if a symbols ends up with several meanings. You might also want to put the more significant dreams and their interpretations in your journal.

This is just the beginning. It is a hint of what you can do with the vast knowledge of the subconscious. Expand on it. You have experienced how easy it is to let it become your servant. You don't have to relive trauma. You don't have to guess. All the knowledge and power of your subconscious mind is yours for the asking now. It is your dearest friend, supporter, ally, mentor, and resource.

Chapter Twenty-Two

The Quality of Life

People have wondered from time immemorial what is life. What is the difference between life and non-life? There is no general agreement.

Can we isolate life? Can we quantify that part of us which is alive? Some scientists believe we can and point to brain waves. They say death comes when brain waves cease and life begins in the womb when brain waves appear. But brain waves are only evidence of life. They don't tell us what life is.

To look at life is like the eye looking at itself. We are it. How could we turn ourselves inside out to look at our Self?

It isn't as hard as as it may seem. You have already started doing it. At each session of *The Fundamental Habit*, you are turning your attention inward and around. You are getting glimpses of your own living Self. You are consciously connecting with your living core. You are tapping the basis of everything: The Unified Field.

It is life. The Unified Field gives rise to awareness, consciousness. When you trace your own consciousness back to its source, The Unified Field, you are looking at your Self. You are looking at life in its fullest state, in its most natural state, and in its most elementary state.

The Unified Field is life in its fullest state because every living entity belongs to it. All life is connected there. All life appears as a single oneness there. Every ounce of life in all of creation is of that field. Now, that is fullness! You can't get any fuller.

The Unified Field is life in its natural state because all the laws of nature emanate from there. All the different forms of life illustrate the play and display of natural law. Although different, each form is part of the whole. All forms and all laws of nature can be traced back to the core, the natural state.

The Unified Field is also life in its most elementary state. Nothing is simpler. From that field, vibration begins. That simple first vibration is the basis for the complex and infinite expressions of creation.

All the qualities of life reside in The Unified Field. These are qualities that every living entity has by virtue of being alive, of being of The Unified Field. To be conscious is to be aware of those qualities. The higher your consciousness, the higher is your awareness of and experience of those qualities.

Our quality of life is directly proportional to the degree to which we are aware of our qualities. And, the degree of awareness is directly proportional to our conscious connection to The Unified Field.

This is why your regular practice of *The Fundamental Habit* is so important. Your quality of life is the issue.

These techniques condition your nervous system to look inward. Your nervous system has that ability, but it hasn't been used for that. Like a muscle you never use, your nerves need to be isolated and practiced regularly. Each time you do *The Fundamental Habit*, you strengthen the nervous system to look inward. After each session, your nervous system is able to be aware of The Unified Field longer and more clearly, but the connection eventually fades. That is why we do the practice twice a day without fail. Twenty minutes twice daily conditions your nervous system to look inward at life itself. Eventually the connection is permanent.

This is not an academic notion. It is a concrete experience. The qualities you want most are developed. They come about without effort, without thinking about them, and without even believing they will. These qualities are inherent to all life. Wherever there is life, there is the basis for the highest quality of life.

And what are these qualities? You already have experienced several creep into your life. Let's look at a few.

Happiness and joy. Yes, that is your nature. Always. Regardless of what is going on around you, you can feel happiness underneath. Happiness and joy can permeate all your moments and every action. There is no reason you can't always feel them. They are qualities of life.

All-knowing intelligence. This whole Course is rooted in this quality. The techniques you have to get answers and guidance prove you have access to nature's intelligence. You need never guess again. You have all the answers you need for knowing your role in preserving order, for evolving with the natural scheme of things, for developing your innate qualities, and for getting in touch with your nature—all you need to know. All-knowing intelligence is a quality of life.

Everywhere present. Now, this one touches on the esoteric. It defies your orientation until you're grounded in The Unified Field. Yes, you are here now but Einstein threw new light on the concept of space and time. At the state of least excitation—at the source of your life—time and space are nowhere and everywhere. Enough said. Eventually you will experience this. Omnipresence is a quality of your life.

Perfection. Life is not random and chaotic. It is orderly and pre-dictable. Nothing happens in life without cause. All of life interacts systematically. That is perfection, and your life is also perfect because perfection is a quality of all life.

Peace. Life is without turmoil. Oh, it might appear to be quite a bat-tleground, but in Truth life is peaceful. Only distorted illusions make it appear otherwise.

Infinite energy. Limitations do not exist for life. Everything is possi-ble. That is a quality of your life.

Abundance. That is the first quality you went after in this Course. Little did you know all these other qualities would catch a piggyback ride. Wealth is your birthright. You can expect it as a quality of life.

This is an opening sampler of qualities. They will appear as perfect health, money, rewarding projects, loving relationships, feelings of happiness, cheery outlooks, peace of mind, skill-in-action, dynamic energy, clarity of thought, gratitude, friendships, fun times, understanding, spontaneity, life supporting habits, balance between work and recreation, to mention a few.

The quality of life is the bottom line for wanting to make money. Now you have techniques that will bring you money plus everything else. It all comes by cultivating an awareness of life. To do this you don't study life. You simply teach your nervous system to look at The Unified Field—to look at life itself in its purest form. The more you are able to look, the more of its inherent qualities surface into your life. It is that simple. The highest quality of life is yours already. Open up to it.

A Word from the Author

Finally, the world is ready. Through the ages Babaji and other Masters have offered techniques to accelerate the growth of awareness. As the atmosphere purified, the techniques became simpler and more effective. This new gift from Babaji shows the progress humankind has made. It is now possible to tune everyone into their eternal vibration with an easy meditation and easy instruction. Finally, the world is ready.

My interest in the potential of our Inner Selves began at an early age. In 1946—when I was 10—I read Baird T. Spalding's Lives and Teachings of the Masters of the Far East. Those three volumes left a profound imprint. I knew there was more that I wasn't experiencing, but I was baffled as to how to reach it.

As so often happens in life, a strange turn of events in 1974 brought a new beginning. I found myself without a law practice, and instead on a quest for my true Self. On that journey I studied Transcendental Meditation from Maharishi Mahesh Yogi and became a TM teacher and a Sidha with the Yoga Sutra techniques. I learned first and second degree Reiki, Mahikari, and Rebirthing.

At a workshop in San Diego called "Teachings of the Inner Christ" I became familiar with Babaji and other Masters. I learned to communicate with them easily and often. One day in Santa Fe, New Mexico I was instructed by Babaji to go into the Rocky Mountains to receive the book Unified: A Course on Truth and Practical Guidance from Babaji. Each day I went into a canyon, got centered and wrote down a chapter. I had no idea beforehand what I would write. Nevertheless, the book flowed perfectly with the simple key for unlocking human potential. All the material on this web site came to me the same way.

For years I've pondered upon my responsibilities toward this knowledge, waiting for the perfect time and perfect vehicle. Well, the time is now. The vehicle is this book.

I am an attorney educated at the University of California at Berkeley. Of course that is hardly a qualification to be a messenger of this precious knowledge, so my role in quite small compared to the thousands of others who are to be the true messengers. Take this knowledge, spread it, and help every person open up to his or her natural qualities.

Roger G. Lanphear